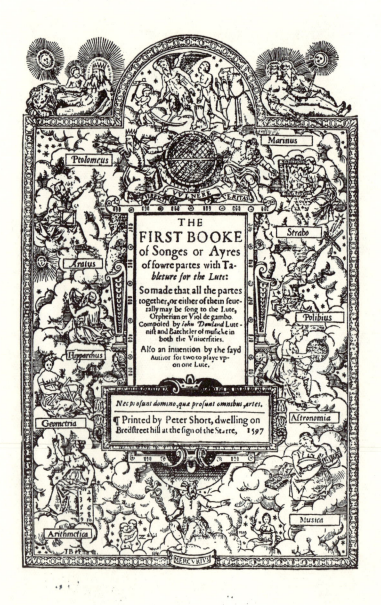

THE
FIRST BOOKE
of Songes or Ayres
of fowre partes with Ta-
bleture for the Lute:

So made that all the partes
together, or either of them seuerally may be song to the Lute,
Orpherian or Viol de gambo.
Compoſed by *iohn Dowland* Lute-
niſt and Batcheler of muſicke in
both the Vniuerſities.

Alſo an inuention by the ſayd
Author for two to playe vp-
on one Lute.

Nec proſunt domino, quæ proſunt omnibus, artes.

¶ Printed by Peter Short, dwelling on
Bredſtreet hill at the ſign of the Starre, 1597

Marinus

Ptolomæus

Strabo

Aratus

Polibius

Hipparchus

Astronomia

Geometria

Musica

Arithmetica

MERCVRIVS

THE
ENGLISH AYRE

By

PETER WARLOCK
(Philip Heseltine)

GREENWOOD PRESS, PUBLISHERS
WESTPORT, CONNECTICUT

123914

Originally published in 1926
by Oxford University Press, London

Reprinted from an original copy in the collections
of the Brooklyn Public Library

First Greenwood Reprinting 1970

Library of Congress Catalogue Card Number 73-109747

SBN 8371-4237-7

Printed in the United States of America

TO THE MEMORY

OF

PHILIP WILSON

CONTENTS

1. Introduction 9
2. John Dowland 21
3. John Danyel 52
4. Robert Jones 63
5. Captain Tobias Hume 82
6. Alfonso Ferrabosco the Younger . . . 90
7. Thomas Campion 98
8. Philip Rosseter 106
9. Cavendish, Greaves, Corkine, Ford, Pilkington, and
   Morley 111
10. Bartlet, Cooper, Maynard, Peerson, Attey, and
    others 121
11. Ayres in Manuscript Collections . . . 125
12. Some Technical Considerations . . . 130
    Chronological Table 137
    Bibliography of Modern Reprints . . . 141

LIST OF ILLUSTRATIONS

Title-page of Dowland's *First Booke of Songes or Ayres*.
First edition, 1597 . . . . *Frontispiece*

'Heere *Philomel*, in silence sits alone.' Poem alluding
to Dowland. From Peacham's *Minerva Britannica*,
1612 45

'Sweet, come away, my darling.' From Robert
Jones's *First Booke of Songs and Ayres*, 1600 . 70–1

Title-page of *The True Petition of Colonel Hume*, 1642 87

The Willow Song—'The poor soul sat sighing by a
sycamore tree.' From B.M. Add. MS. 15117 . 127

I

Introduction

WHEN Mr. Leopold Bloom, wandering home through the streets of Dublin in the small hours of the 16th of June 1904, grew lyrical over the music of Mercadante and Meyerbeer, *Martha* and pseudo-Mozart, his companion, Stephen Dedalus, 'launched out into praises of Shakespeare's songs, at least of in or about that period, the lutenist Dowland who lived in Fetter Lane near Gerard the herbalist, and Farnaby and son with their *dux* and *comes* conceits and Byrd (William), who played the virginals in the Queen's Chapel or anywhere else he found them and one Tomkins who made toys or ayres and John Bull '.

Exactly how Stephen Dedalus contrived to acquaint himself with the works of Dowland twenty years ago is not very clear ; for although he would have found plenty of Byrd, Farnaby, and Tomkins in the Fitzwilliam Virginal Book—that precious miscellany of Elizabethan keyboard music which, long known to students of musical manuscripts by the quite erroneous title of ' Queen Elizabeth's Virginal Book ', was at length printed and published in 1899—the songs of Dowland and his fellow lutenists were still inaccessible to the general public. It is a remarkable thing that all the various other kinds of music that were flourishing in England at the end of the sixteenth and the beginning of the seventeenth centuries—the Mass, the Anglican service, the anthem, the madrigal, the instrumental fantasia, and the various dance forms—should have received attention at the hands of modern editors and historians before the accompanied song or ayre, the simplest of all musical forms then in vogue and the one most likely to win immediate popularity in another age. The exquisite lyrics from the song-books which were hailed with such delight when A. H. Bullen first published them in the 'eighties, were all taken direct from the music-books in which they were originally printed ; and these song-books are, for the majority of the lyrics, the only sources. But until the last few years the music associated with these poems has been strangely neglected, and musicians are only just beginning to realize that we have here a body of English song of which any country at any period of history might well be proud.

Song, or rather accompanied tune, is for us so much the simplest and most universal form of music that it is a little difficult to realize that, historically speaking, it is a fairly recent development. Plain-song and folk-song come down to us from remote antiquity, but no one knows with any real certainty when it was that the European mind first stumbled upon that characteristic which still so sharply differentiates Western from Eastern music—namely, the embellishment of one tune by the addition of another. In the music of most Oriental countries any embellishments that may be added to a tune by voices or instruments are either purely rhythmic, or, in so far as they are melodic at all, simply consist of variations on the tune itself. The musical line traced by an Eastern singer accompanying himself on an instrument is apt to suggest to Western ears a picture of two dogs following the same scent ; both keep to the same general direction, but from time to time one or other of them will dart a little way off the track and quickly return to it. But in such music there can be no question of harmony as we understand it, or even of definite melodic intervals between one voice and another, or between voice and instrument. The Middle Ages gave Europe both harmony and counterpoint, in embryonic form : harmony in the doubling of a melody at a given interval which was con- sidered harmonious in itself, counterpoint in the florid descants which were improvised, with varying degrees of skill, by individual singers over a *canto fermo* of plain chant in the church services. It is probable that what is considered to be the earliest form of harmony—the *Organum* of Hucbald in the ninth century, which consists simply of doubling a melody in fourths and fifths—was the result of mathematical rather than purely musical thought, an acoustic rather than an aesthetic phenomenon. It seems likely that from the wild random experiments of the improvisers there emerged a general preference of the ear for the sound of certain intervals sung in sequence, such as the third and sixth, with which was combined a liking for independence of movement in the two or more voices which sang together. We certainly find these two elements, the one harmonic, the other contrapuntal, in the earliest piece of concerted music which can still be heard with aesthetic enjoyment at the present time—the remarkable canon or round on a recurring ground-bass, *Sumer is icumen in*, which, though long attributed to the early fifteenth century by the historians of music, has been proved by palaeographers, on the evidence of the manuscript in which it has come down to us, to date from the fourth or fifth decade of the thirteenth century. The question arises : did recognition of certain intervals as being more consonant than others determine the early efforts of those musicians who sought to set one tune in harmonious relation with another, or to dove-tail sections of one tune into each other in a round or canon, or were these intervals or points of repose discovered, more or less accidentally, in the course of long years of extemporary descanting ?

The question whether harmony is a development of counterpoint or vice versa is as difficult as that of the precedence of chicken or egg. It would be possible to construct a fairly convincing view of European musical history on the familiar antithetical basis of Apollo and Dionysus, classic and romantic, from study of the interaction of these two elements of music alone ; but such a view would not be wholly convincing. Melody was with us before either of these elements was dreamed of, and the most that counterpoint can do is to develop, as the most that harmony can do is to reinforce, melody. Melody is the basis of all music, whether it be polyphonic in structure, as in Masses, madrigals, and fugues, or harmonic as in any plain straight-forward accompanied tune. The history of the development of counterpoint through the Middle Ages has been preserved for us in a series of musical manuscripts and treatises : the history of tune comes down to us only in scattered fragments. The explanation is simple enough, since tunes can be carried in the head and passed from mouth to mouth, while Masses and motets must be written down to be remembered. It is easy to realize that in olden as in more recent times, counterpoint, which must be learned with labour out of books, came to be regarded as intrinsically more important than melody born of spontaneous inspiration. The bards and minstrels who went about the country singing tunes to the accompaniment of their harps or lutes or kindred instruments were looked down upon by the ecclesiastics as lewd fellows of the baser sort, and their works are now, un-happily, forgotten, while many a dull Mass of their clerical contemporaries has been preserved for us in a monkish manu-script. ' Honoured and revered during a barbarous age,' says William Dauney, ' it was the singular fate of this class of men [that is, the itinerant secular musicians], at a period when the world became more enlightened and the arts which they pro-fessed better known and more highly cultivated, to be thrust into juxtaposition with the very dregs and refuse of society, and stigmatised as rogues, vagabonds, and sturdy beggars.'

The history of secular music in Europe during the Middle Ages is shrouded in obscurity. But it is quite evident from the few gleams of light that shine out of the dark period between the end of the twelfth century and the beginning of the sixteenth, that secular practices played an important part in the development

of the resources of musical composition. By the beginning of
the thirteenth century the troubadours in France had brought
the art of setting highly organized forms of poetry to expressive
melodies to a very considerable degree of perfection. Now
troubadour poetry, as Dr. Chaytor points out in his excellent little
book on *The Troubadours,* was the outcome and fine flower of
folk-poetry ; and we may perhaps assume that their music was
not wholly uninfluenced by folk-music. ' The singer ', Dr. Chaytor
tells us, ' accompanied himself upon a stringed instrument (Viula),
or was accompanied by other performers ; various forms of wind
instruments were also in use. Apparently the accompaniment
was in unison with the singer ; part-writing or contrapuntal
music was unknown at the troubadour period.' There is, however, no direct evidence of the nature of the accompaniments
employed by the troubadours ; on the other hand, there is
evidence of the use of polyphony in the popular music of the
countryside in the last years of the twelfth century. Giraldus
Cambrensis, in his *Description of Wales,* tells us very definitely
that the Welsh ' did not sing in unison like the inhabitants of
other countries, but in many different parts, so that in a company
of singers you might hear as many parts and voices as there are
performers . He continues :

' In the northern districts of Britain, beyond the Humber, and
on the borders of Yorkshire, the inhabitants make use of the same
kind of symphonious harmony but with less variety ; singing only
in two parts, one murmuring in the bass, the other warbling in the
treble. Neither of the two nations has acquired this peculiarity
by art, but by long habit, which has rendered it natural and familiar ;
and the practice is now so firmly rooted in them, that it is unusual
to hear a simple and single melody well sung ; and, what is still
more wonderful, the children, even from their infancy, sing in the
same manner. As the English in general do not adopt this mode
of singing, only those in the northern counties, I believe that it
was from the Danes and Norwegians, by whom these parts of the

island were more frequently invaded, and held longer under their dominion, that the natives contracted their mode of singing.'

Giraldus speaks also of the instrumental music of the Welsh and Irish of this period, which he describes as ' producing consonance from the rapidity of seemingly discordant touches '.

It is evident that the music of the Church was considerably affected by the style of popular music in vogue about this time, for in 1322 we find Pope John XXII denouncing the invasion of church music by secular influences, and ordering a strict return to the old methods of *organum* sanctioned by ecclesiastical authority. So it seems that, in respect of harmonic development, secular practice was well ahead of ecclesiastical theory at this time. Less than twenty years after this papal decree, the Church itself admitted the practice of singing in *faux-bourdon*, or sequences of thirds and sixths ; and these, as we see from the evidence of *Sumer is icumen in*, had been in use in secular music for over a hundred years. Many delightful specimens of fourteenth- and fifteenth-century English secular song have been transcribed from contemporary manuscripts and printed by Sir John Stainer in his *Early Bodleian Music*, and some of these seem to provide definite evidence of instrumental accompaniment, and even of instrumental interludes between the vocal phrases. In France polyphony in secular song reached a very high point of development in the works of Guillaume de Machault in the first half of the fourteenth century. The importance of this composer's work is frequently overlooked by musical historians, for the typical historian's reason that, as Dr. Walker puts it in his *History of Music in England*, his ' notions of harmonic propriety are not correlatable, as Dunstable's are, with modern methods '. Now Dunstable, who flourished exactly a century later, is often referred to as the father, or even as the inventor, of counterpoint ; but the works of Machault, together with the other evidences of secular music already referred to, would seem to prove quite conclusively that there were all through the Middle Ages two distinct musical traditions and two distinct musical styles, the one secular and for the most part oral, the other ecclesiastical ; that these two traditions were perpetually at variance with each other ; and that, as nearly all our documentary evidence of musical practices derives from the ecclesiastical tradition, musical historians have hitherto given us a completely one-sided picture of the music of the Middle Ages.

The fifteenth century witnessed immense developments in contrapuntal resources, based upon the ecclesiastical tradition, and in the works of its greatest master, Josquin Després, we see clearly defined the harmonic principles which were to determine the course of the next two centuries' musical developments. In this period it seems probable that secular music acquired as much from the methods of the Church as the Church had formerly acquired from it, but what remained specifically the property of secular music was the metrical tune, which, in nine cases out of ten, probably owed its origin to the dance. In the fifteenth century we see the principle of constructing a movement on the polyphonic basis of an unrhythmical plain-chant extended to the point of substituting for the plain-chant a metrical tune of obviously popular origin, such as the beautiful *Westron Wynde* melody, round which the English composers Tye, Shepherd, and Taverner wove their Masses of that name. In these works we have the germ of the accompanied melody. Although in polyphonic music all voices are of equal importance, no one part predominating over another for any length of time, it is but a step, once a rhythmically self-subsistent melody has been taken to provide the framework of a contrapuntal composition, to construct a musical composition as a frame or setting for some given melody. Quite early in the sixteenth century the French had mastered the art of setting dance-tunes for four or five voices in this fashion, and it was soon discovered that whatever could be sung could also be played on stringed or other instruments ; or perhaps some might sing and some might play, so long as all the notes were sounded in one way or the other. But there were certain instruments which, unlike the human voice, were capable of sounding more than one note at once ; and as their use was extended, the conception of music as being, so to speak, two-dimensional, grew clearer in men's minds. Though a piece of music was primarily constructed as a series of horizontal lines tending in ordered relation towards an appointed end, it became apparent that there was a vertical as well as an horizontal aspect to music, and that by drawing a series of imaginary vertical lines across the horizontal texture of a piece of music at regular intervals, you could, as it were, gather up the notes in handfuls : and these handfuls were what we now call *chords*. They were not at that time thought of as mere handfuls of notes ; composers continued to think their music horizontally, but for purposes of convenience they would often gather up three or four strands of music as best they could so as to bring them under the hands of a lutenist or virginal player, leaving only the tune or principal part to be sung. Sometimes, too, compositions originally intended for several voices were arranged so that they could be sung by one voice to the accompaniment of a lute. Thus in 1536 we find Willaert publishing a book of twenty-two madrigals by Verdelot in an arrangement for solo voice and lute. But we have now already entered the period when songs were definitely composed for publication in this form, for in 1536 there appeared the first book of accompanied solo songs that ever was printed.

This was the *Libro de Musica de Vihuela de Mano. Intitulado El Maestro*, by Don Luis Milan, of Valencia.[1] The title-page of this book represents Orpheus, surrounded by all kinds of animals

---

[1] For an excellent account of Milán and his contemporaries, with several musical examples, see J. B. Trend, *Luis Milan and the Vihuelistas* (Hispanic Notes and Monographs, XI).

and playing the lute, and the picture is encircled by these words :
' El grande Orpheo primero inventor, por quien la vihuela parece
en el mundo. Si el fue el primero, no fue sin segundo.' (' The
great Orpheus, first inventor by whom the lute came into the
world. If he was the first, he was not without a second.')

The lute was an instrument of Arab origin, its name being
derived from the Arabic *Al-'ūd*. Spain was probably the first
European country where it was extensively used, and the technique
of the Spanish lutenists is said to have been introduced into Italy
by the musicians attached to the court of the princes of Aragon,
who had been kings of Sicily since the end of the thirteenth
century. Milan's *vihuela* was something between the English
lute and the present Spanish guitar, the qualification *de mano*
being added to distinguish it from the *vihuela de arco*, which was
a viol. Although *El Maestro* is actually the first book of accompanied songs that was ever published, Milan's work by no means
represents the tentative beginnings of a new and experimental
art. On the contrary, he seems to have been a technically accom-
plished composer, and his lute parts, so far from being mere
approximations to vocal polyphony, show a real feeling for instrumental style and the capabilities of a plucked-string instrument.
As Gevaert says : ' L'œuvre de Milan contenue dans le *Maestro*
ne peut donc représenter à nos yeux le début d'un genre d'art,
mais son efflorescence. Elle implique une tradition technique
déjà solidement établie, et suppose conséquemment une succession
d'artistes habiles remontant à plusieurs générations.'

Milan's book was soon followed by other publications of similar
character in Spain, and soon after 1550 books of lute music began to
appear also in France. Of these, perhaps the most remarkable was
the *Instruction de partir toute musique des huit divers tons en tablature
de luth*, which Adrian Le Roy and Robert Ballard published in
1557. This was translated into English and published in 1568
under the title of *A briefe and easye instruction to learne the table-*

B

ture, and another translation of the same work appeared in 1574. Two little songs in William Barley's *Newe book of tabliture* (1596) are actually the first examples of this kind of music to be published in England, but in the following year appeared John Dowland's *First Booke of Songes or Ayres of fowre partes with Tableture for the Lute,* and with this book the period of the English Ayre may be said to open. It must be added, however, that several of the *Songes of three, fower, and five voyces* by Thomas Whythorne (1571) are indistinguishable in form from the ayres of the later composers. Although designed for unaccompanied voices, they are indisputably ayres in that the highest voice is given a definite tune to sing while the others have subsidiary accompanying parts. Whythorne, who has been consistently abused by musical historians, was no mean composer, and such songs as ' It doth belong more in good right ', ' As thy shadow ', and ' Give not thy mind to heaviness ' are worthy to rank with the best of the later ayres.

Before proceeding to a consideration of the individual composers and their works, something should be said about the manner in which the song-books were printed. Unlike the madrigals of the period which were printed in small quarto volumes, a separate part in each volume and only one in each, the ayres were printed in folio books. On the left-hand page, as the book lay open, was the principal voice-part with the words and the accompaniment for the lute set out in tablature notation immediately below it. On the right-hand page were the additional parts for alto, tenor, and bass, or in some cases for the bass viol alone, so printed that if the book lay open upon a table a singer might sit at each side of it and read his part. The ayres, for all their careful construction, were so made that, although one person alone might render them quite adequately to his own accompaniment on the lute, he might be reinforced by one, two, or three other singers, each of whom would have a separate part to sing. The tablature notation indicated not the notes that were to be played, but the strings and frets of the lute on which the fingers were to be placed to produce them. It was written on a six-line stave, as the lute had six principal strings, with sometimes an additional bass string or two which was notated below the bottom line of the stave. The six principal strings were tuned thus :

Example 1.

The notes of the sixth string were written in the lowest space of the stave, those of the fifth in the second space, and so on. On the neck of the lute frets were placed in such a way that by stopping the strings fret by fret an ascending chromatic sequence of notes was produced ; thus the open string sounding G would, if stopped at the first fret sound G sharp, if stopped at the second, A, at the third, B flat, and so on. In tablature notation the open string was always called a, the first fret b, the second c, &c. Note-values were indicated by signs placed over the stave, each one remaining in force till contradicted by another. An example will make this clearer than any description :

Example 2.

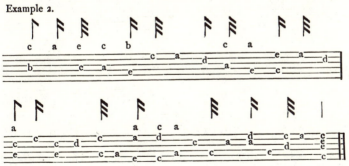

This passage interpreted in terms of ordinary staff notation becomes :

Example 3.

But as the lute suggested more than it actually sounded, the structure of the music is best indicated in transcription by observing the moving parts of which it is composed. So the body of the passage of which we have quoted the skeleton is seen to be :

Example 4.

Other points about notation and the problems connected with its transcription will be discussed in a later chapter, when we have made a general survey of the music itself.

John Dowland

The few facts definitely known about the life of the greatest of English song-writers may be stated summarily in a very small space. The detail with which they are surrounded will be given in quotations from Dowland's own writings (in the prefaces and dedications of his books) and from those of his contemporaries who referred to him.

1563 John Dowland born.

1580 Goes to France in the service of the English ambassador. Is converted to the Roman Catholic faith.

1582 Returns to England.

1588 Takes degree of Mus.Bac. at Oxford, in company with Thomas Morley.

1592 Contributes harmonized tunes to Este's *Whole Book of Psalmes*.

1594 Fails to obtain position as one of Queen Elizabeth's musicians on account of his Catholicism. Leaves England and travels from court to court in Germany and Italy.

1595 Writes long autobiographical letter to Sir Robert Cecil, in which he confesses his reconversion to Protestantism.

1596 Some of his lute-music printed without his permission by William Barley in *A new Booke of Tabliture*.

1597 Publishes his *First Booke of Songes or Ayres*.

1598 Receives appointment as instrumentalist at the court of King Christian IV of Denmark.

His name coupled with Edmund Spenser's in Richard Barnefield's sonnet. Contributes laudatory poem to Farnaby's Canzonets.

1599 Contributes laudatory poem to Richard Alison's *Psalmes of David in meter*.

1600 His *Second Booke of Songs or Ayres* published in London, with a dedicatory preface written from Elsinore in Denmark.

Second edition of the *First Book of Songs* printed.

1601 Sent to England to purchase musical instruments for the Danish court. Decorated by the King of Denmark.

1603 His *Third and Last Booke of Songs or Aires* published in London.

1605   His *Lachrimae or Seaven Teares figured in Seaven Passionate Pavans . . .
       set forth for the Lute, Viols, or Violons, in five parts*, published in
       London.

1606   February.   Dismissed from his post at the Danish court.
       Third edition of the *First Book of Songs* printed.

1608   Fourth edition of the *First Book of Songs* printed.

1609   Publishes his translation of *Andreas Ornithoparcus his Micrologus or
       Introduction containing the Art of Singing.*
       Living in Fetter Lane, London.

1610   Contributes some ' Observations belonging to Lute-playing ' to his son
       Robert's *Varietie of Lute-Lessons*, and three songs to Robert's *Musicall
       Banquet.*

1612   Publishes *A Pilgrimes Solace.*   Lutenist to Lord Walden.
       Henry Peacham's poem in *Minerva Britannica* alludes to the neglect
       of Dowland in his own country.
       Appointed one of King James's musicians for the lutes.

1613   Fifth edition of the *First Book of Songs* printed.

1614   Contributes two hymns to Sir William Leighton's *Teares or Lamenta-
       cions of a Sorrowfull Soule.*

1626. 21 January.   John Dowland died in London.

An article by Dr. W. H. Grattan Flood, published in *The
Gentleman's Magazine* in 1906, tells us that the composer was
born at Christmas time in the year 1562 in Ireland, possibly at
Dalkey, Co. Dublin, and that his father's name was John Dowlan
(or Dolan) ; but as the evidence supporting this statement is
slender, it must be accepted with a certain amount of reserve, as
must also Dr. Grattan Flood's assertions that Dowland was a ' very
intimate ' and ' intrinsic friend ' of Shakespeare, much as we
should like to believe it.   Dowland says, in the ' Observations
belonging to lute-playing ', that he was born thirty years after
Hans Gerle's book was printed.   This book was the *Tabulatur
auf die Lauten*, which appeared in 1533.   This statement as to
the year of Dowland's birth is corroborated by his remark in the
preface to *A Pilgrim's Solace* (1612) that he was then ' entered
into the 50th year of his age '.

If there is any positive evidence proving that Dowland the composer was in fact the son of the John Dowlan of Dalkey who died in 1577, or that he is to be identified with the John Dowland who was in commons for nine weeks in 1604–5 at Trinity College, Dublin, such evidence has not hitherto been published. The dedication of one of the songs in *A Pilgrim's Solace*, ' To my loving Country-man Mr. John Forster the younger, Merchant of Dublin in Ireland ', has been regarded as evidence that Dowland considered himself an Irishman. But, on the other hand, the address to the reader in the same book begins with the words, ' Worthy Gentlemen and my loving Countrymen ', which would seem rather to refer to the British public in general, to whom the composer was seeking to reintroduce himself after several years' absence in foreign countries.

It seems likely that the first syllable of Dowland's name was pronounced as rhyming with *blue* and not with *cow*. It is spelt *Dowland* in the first, second, and third Books of Ayres, and *Douland* (with or without a final *e*) in *A Pilgrim's Solace*, in the translation of Ornithoparcus, in the *Musical Banquet*, and in the autograph letter to Sir Robert Cecil, while in one of the Danish court pay-lists it appears as *Dulanntt*.

In the autograph signature which Dowland attached to a few bars of his ' Lachrimae ' as a contribution to the *Album Amicorum* of Johann Cellarius of Nuremberg, the name is spelt *Doland*, and this version is used by Campion in his Latin epigrams addressed to the composer. A piece entitled ' Joannis Dulandi Fantasia ' appears in a German manuscript of lute-music belonging to the seventeenth century.

Dowland's letter to Sir Robert Cecil, written from Nuremberg on the 10th of November 1595, contains so much interesting autobiographical detail that it must be quoted in full. It was first printed by the Historical MSS. Commission in 1894 in the Calendar of the MSS. of the Marquis of Salisbury, preserved at

Hatfield House, Hertfordshire, Part V, and an extensive commentary on its contents, with especial reference to the identity of the subsidiary characters mentioned in it, was published by Mr. W. Barclay Squire in the *Musical Times* in 1896–7.

John Doulande to Sir Robert Cecil

'Right honourable, as I have been most bound unto your honour, so I most humbly desire your honour to pardon my boldness and make my choice of your honour to let you understand my bounden duty and desire of God's preservation of my most dear Sovereign Queen and country, whom I beseech God ever to bless and to confound all their enemies what and whomsoever. Fifteen years since I was in France, servant to Sir Henry Cobham, who was ambassador for the Queen's Majesty, and lay in Paris, where I fell acquainted with one Smith, a priest, and one Morgan, sometimes of Her Majesty's chapel, one Vestigan who brake out of England, being apprehended, and one Moris, a Welshman, that was our porter, who is at Rome. These men thrust many idle toys into my head of religion, saying that the Papists' was the truth and ours in England all false; and I, being but young, their fair words over reached me and I believed with them. Within 2 years after I came into England where I saw men of that faction condemned and executed, which I thought was great injustice, taking religion for the only cause, and when my best friends would persuade me I would not believe them. Then in time passing one Mr. Johnson died, and I became an humble suitor for his place (thinking myself most worthiest) wherein I found many good and honourable friends that spake for me, but I saw that I was like to go without it, and that any might have preferment but I. Whereby I began to sound the cause and guessed that my religion was my hindrance; whereupon, my mind being troubled, I desired to get beyond the seas, which I durst not attempt without licence from some of the Privy Council, for fear of being taken, and so have extreme punishment. And according as I desired there came a letter to me out of Germany from the Duke of Brunswick. Whereupon I spake to your honour and to my lord of Essex, who willingly gave me both your hands (for which I would be glad if there were any

service in me that your honours could command). When I came
to the Duke of Brunswick he used me kindly and gave me a rich
chain of gold, 23£ in money, with velvet and satin and gold lace
to make me apparell, with promise that if I would serve him he
would give me as much as any prince in the world. From thence
I went to the Lantgrave of Hessen, who gave me the greatest
welcome that might be for one of my quality, who sent a ring
into England to my wife, valued at 20£ sterling, and gave me
a great standing cup with a cover gilt, full of dollars, with many
great offers for my service. From thence I had great desire to see
Italy and came to Venice and from thence to Florence, where I
played before the Duke and got great favours ; and one evening
I was walking upon the *piazzo* in Florence, a gentleman told me
that he espied an English priest, and that his name was Skidmore,
and son and heir to Sir John Skidmore of the Court. So, I being
intended to go to Rome to study with a famous musician named
Luca Marenzio stepped to this Mr. Skidmore, the priest, and
asked him if he were an Englishman, and he told me yea, and
whose son he was. And I telling him my name, he was very glad
to see me. So I told him I would go to Rome and desired his
help for my safety ; for, said I, if they should mistake me there
my fortune were hard, for I have been thrust off of all good fortunes, because I am a Catholic, at home ; for I heard that her
Majesty, being spoke to for me, said I was a man to serve any
prince in the world, but I was an obstinate papist. Whereupon
he answered, " Mr. Dowlande, if it be not so, make her words
true." So, in further talk, we spake of priests, and I told him
that I did not think it true that any priests (as we said in England)
would kill the Queen, or one go about to touch her finger, and,
said I, " Whatsoever my religion be, I will neither meddle nor
make with anything there done, so that they do not anything
against the Queen." Whereunto he answered that I spake as
a good subject to her Majesty. But, said he, in Rome you shall
hear Englishmen, your own countrymen, speak most hardly of
her and wholly seek to overthrow her and all England ; and
those be the Jesuits, said he, who are of the Spanish faction.
Moreover, said he, we have many jars with them ; and withal
wished to God the Queen were a Catholic. And, said he, to
defend my country against the Spaniards I would come into

England and bear a pike on my shoulders. Among our talk, he told me that he had order to attach divers English gentlemen, and that he had been three years England (*sic*). So I brought him to his lodging door, where he told me that there was 9 priests come from Rome to go for England. He came but the day before to Florence; and, I think, they came all together. He told me that he would stay there in the town and study in an abbey called *Sancta Maria Novella*, and that he must keep in for a month, and that he would write letters of me to Rome which I should receive very shortly. But I heard not of him in a month after. And then there came two friars to my lodgings, the one was an Englishman named Balye, a Yorkshireman. The next day after my speech with Skidmore, I dined with my lord Gray and divers other gentlemen, whom I told of my speech with Skidmor, giving them warning. Whereupon my lord Gray went to Siena and the rest dispersed themselves. Moreover, I told my lord Gray, howsoever I was for religion, if I did perceive anything in Rome that either touched Her Majesty or the State of England, I would give notice of it though it were the loss of my life. Which he liked well, and bade me keep that secret. This Friar Baylie, before named, delivered me a letter which I have here sent unto your honour, which letter I brake open before Mr. Josias Bodly, and showed what was written in it to him, and divers other. After this, this Friar Bayly told me he had received letters from Rome to hasten me forward, and told me that my discontentment was known at Rome, and that I should have a large pension of the Pope, and that his Holiness and all the Cardinals would make wonderful much of me. Thereupon I told him of my wife and children, how to get them to me. Whereunto he told me that I should have acquaintance with such as should bring them over, if she had any willingness, or else they would lose their lives; for there came those into England for such purposes; for, quoth he, Mr. Skidmore brought out of England, at his last being there, xvij persons, both men and women, for which the Bishop weeps, when he sees him, for joy. After my departure I called to mind our conference, and got me by myself and wept heartily to see my fortune so hard that I should become servant to the greatest enemy of my prince, country, wife, children and friends, for want. And to make me like themselves, God knoweth I never loved treason nor treachery, nor never knew of any, nor never heard any mass in England, which I find is great abuse of the people, for, on my soul, I understand it not. Wherefore I have reformed myself to live according to her Majesty's laws, as I was born under her Highness, and that, most humbly, I do crave pardon, protesting if there were any ability in me I would be most ready to make amends. At Bolona I met with ij men, the one named Pierce, an Irishman, the other named Dracot. They are gone, both, to Rome. In Venice I heard an Italian say that he marvelled that King Philip had never a good friend in England, that with his dagger would despatch the Queen's Majesty ; " but ", said he, " God suffers her in the end to give her the greater overthrow." Right honourable, this have I written that her Majesty may know the villany of these most wicked priests and Jesuits and to beware of them. I thank God I have both forsaken them and their religion, which tendeth to nothing but destruction. Thus I beseech God, night and day, to bless and defend the Queen's Majesty, and to confound all her enemies, and to preserve your honour and all the rest of her Majesty's most honourable Privy Council. I think that Skidmore and the other priests are all in England ; for he staid not at Florence, as he said he would to me, and Friar Baylie told me that he was gone into France to study the law. At Venice and all along as I come into Germany say that the King of Spain is making great preparation to come for England this next summer, where, if it pleased your honour to advise me, by my poor wife, I would most willingly lose my life against them. Most humbly beseeching your honour to pardon my ill writing, and worse inditing, and to think that I desire to serve my country and hope to hear of your good opinion of me.'

The Mr. Johnson referred to was John Johnson who died about 1594. Richard Verstegan, the priest, was also a poet, author of *The Restitution of Decayed Intelligence* and other works.

Henry Peacham in *The Compleat Gentleman* speaks very highly of the musical abilities of Landgrave of Hessen. After mentioning

King Henry VIII and Gesualdo, Prince of Venosa, as musicians of noble birth, he continues :

' But above others, who carrieth away the palm for excellency, not only in music, but in whatsoever is to be wished in a brave prince, is the yet living Maurice Landgrave of Hessen, of whose own composition I have seen eight or ten several sets of Motets and solemn music set purposely for his own chapel, where for the greater honour of some festival, and many times for his recreation only he is his own organist.'

A pavan for the lute, composed by the Landgrave, is included in *Varietie of Lute Lessons*. This, Robert Dowland tells us, ' was sent to my father, with this inscription following, and written with his Grace's own hand : *Mauritius Landgravius Hessiae fecit in honorem Joanni Doulandi Anglorum Orphei.*'

Already in 1595 Dowland had achieved a great reputation as a musician. A letter from ' John Scudamore, Priest, to Nicholas Fitzherbert at Rome ', dated the 7th of July of that year from Florence (also printed in the Salisbury Papers), begs Fitzherbert to do all he can for Mr. Douland, whose ' exquisiteness upon the lute ' and ' cunning in music ' will have come to his ears long ago. ' I do assure you ', continues Scudamore, ' *in verbo sacerdotis* that he is no meddler but rather inclined to the good, and only for the fame of Lucca Emorentiana and love of music has undertaken this voyage.'

' Lucca Emorentiana ' is, of course, Luca Marenzio, who evidently held Dowland in high esteem.

But it was the publication in 1597 of the first book of songs, which ran through five editions in the next sixteen years, that established Dowland's reputation as a composer both here and abroad. The full title of this work is :

' The First Booke of Songes or Ayres of fowre partes with Tableture for the Lute :

' So made that all the partes together, or either of them seuerally may be song to the Lute, Orpherian, or Viol de gambo. Composed by John Dowland, Lutenist and Batcheler of Musicke in both the Universities.

' Printed by Peter Short the assigne of Th. Morley & are to be sold at the Signe of the Starre on Bred-street Hill. 1597.'

This ambiguously worded description evidently means that the ayres might be sung either by four voices in harmony, or by one voice singing the tune, to the accompaniment of the lute, &c. It would be ridiculous to suppose that the loose wording (obviously the work of the printer and not the composer) implied that one or other of the inner parts should be sung by itself with instrumental accompaniment, for although the lute part doubles more or less exactly the supporting harmonies of the three lower voices, it never by any chance includes the air itself.

The book is dedicated to Sir George Carey, and is prefaced by a Latin epigram of Thomas Campion (in which the composer is addressed, in the vocative case, as Dolandi) and an address ' to the Courteous Reader '.

' How hard an enterprise it is in this skilful and curious age to commit our private labours to the public view, mine own disability and others' hard success do too well assure me : and were it not for that love I bear to the true lovers of music, I had concealed these my first fruits, which how they will thrive with your taste I know not, howsoever the greater part of them might have been ripe enough by their age. The courtly judgment I hope will not be severe against them, being itself a party, and those sweet springs of humanity (I mean our two famous universities) will entertain them for his sake whom they have already graced and as it were enfranchised in the ingenuous profession of music, which from my childhood I have ever aimed at, sundry times leaving my native country the better to attain so excellent a science.

' About sixteen years past I travelled the chiefest parts of France, a nation furnished with great variety of music. But lately, being of a more confirmed judgment, I bent my course toward the famous provinces of Germany, where I found both excellent masters and most honourable patrons of music : namely, those two miracles of this age for virtue and magnificence, Henry Julio, Duke of Brunswick, and learned Maritius Lantzgrave of Hessen, of whose princely virtues and favours towards me I can never speak sufficiently. Neither can I forget the kindness of Alexandro Horologio, a right learned master of music, servant to the royal Prince the Lantzgrave of Hessen, and Gregorio Howet, lutenist to the magnificent Duke of Brunswick, both whom I name as well for their love to me as also for their excellency in their faculties. Thus having spent some months in Germany, to my great admiration of that worthy country, I passed over the Alps into Italy, where I found the cities furnished with all good arts, but especially music. What favour and estimation I had in Venice, Padua, Genoa, Ferrara, Florence, and divers other places I willingly suppress, lest I should any way seem partial in mine own endeavours. Yet can I not dissemble the great content I found in the proffered amity of the most famous Luca Marenzio, whose sundry letters I received from Rome, and one of them, because it is but short, I have thought good to set down, not thinking it any disgrace to be proud of the judgment of so excellent a man.

' Not to stand too long upon my travels, I will only name that worthy master Giovanni Crochio, Vice-Master of the Chapel of S. Marks at Venice, with whom I had familiar conference. And thus what experience I could gather abroad I am now ready to practise at home if I may but find encouragement in my first essays. There have been divers lute lessons of mine lately printed without my knowledge, false and unperfect, but I purpose shortly myself to set forth the choicest of all my lessons in print, and also an introduction for fingering, with other books of songs, whereof this is the first ; and as this finds favour with you, so shall I be affected to labour in the rest.

Farewell,
JOHN DOWLAND.'

The letter of Marenzio which Dowland prints runs as follows :

' Molto magnifico Signior mio osservandissimo. Per una lettera del Signior Alberigo Maluezi ho inteso quanto con cortese affetto

si mostri desideroso di essermi congionto d'amicitia, dove infinita-
mente la ringratio di questo suo buon' animo, offerendo megli
all' incontro se in alcuna cosa la posso servire, poi che gli meriti
delle sue infinite virtù, & qualità meritano che ogni uno & me
l'ammirino & osservino, & per fine di questo le bascio le mani.
Di Roma a' 13. di Luglio. 1595 D.V.S. Affettionatissimo servitore,
Luca Marenzio.'

The language is stilted and the style affected, but the gist of
the letter is that Marenzio greatly appreciates Dowland's desire
to make his acquaintance, and professes his readiness to do any
thing that may be of service to him during his travels in Italy.
In thus paying homage to an English musician of genius, Marenzio
was reciprocating the appreciation of his own works in our country,
where, a few years previously, a number of his madrigals had been
republished with English words, which seems to show that they
had already achieved considerable popularity here in their original
form. And as late as 1622 Henry Peacham could still write :
' For delicious air and sweet invention in Madrigals, Luca Marenzio excelleth all other whosoever.'

Visiting Ferrara in 1594 or 1595, Dowland may perhaps have
made the acquaintance of Gesualdo, who was at that time living
at the court of the Estensi at Ferrara ; in any case, he must have
heard some of Gesualdo's music there, for the first and second
books of the prince's madrigals had just been printed at the ducal
press, and were attracting a great deal of attention in that excep-
tionally musical city.

From the title-page and from the address to the reader it
appears that before this first book of ayres was printed Dowland
had taken a musical degree at Cambridge as well as at Oxford,
but there is no further record of his having done so. In Thomas
Tomkins's *Songs of 3. 4. 5. and 6. parts* (1622), and in the Audit
Office Accounts from 1623 onwards, he is described as *Doctor*
Dowland. Possibly some foreign university conferred this degree

on him, for he does not appear to have proceeded to a doctorate either at Oxford or at Cambridge.

In 1598 Richard Barnfield published his *Encomium of Lady Pecunia ; or the Praise of Money : the complaint of Poetrie for the Death of Liberalitie*, in which appeared a sonnet referring to Dowland, which was at one time attributed to Shakespeare on account of its inclusion by William Jaggard, the printer, in his piracy known as *The Passionate Pilgrim* in 1599.

> If music and sweet poetry agree,
> As they must needs, the sister and the brother,
> Then must the love be great 'twixt thee and me,
> Because thou lov'st the one, and I the other.
> Dowland to thee is dear, whose heavenly touch
> Upon the lute doth ravish human sense ;
> Spenser to me, whose deep conceit is such
> As, passing all conceit, needs no defence.
> Thou lov'st to hear the sweet melodious sound
> That Phoebus' lute, the queen of music, makes ;
> And I in deep delight am chiefly drown'd
> Whenas himself to singing he betakes.
> One god is god of both, as poets feign ;
> One knight loves both, and both in thee remain.

In the same year Dowland contributed a very Chestertonian little poem to Giles Farnaby's book of Canzonets to four voices :

> Thou only shalt have Phyllis,
> Only thou fit (without all further gloses)
> Crowned to be with everlasting roses,
> With roses and with lilies,
> And with daffadowndillies :
> But thy songs sweeter are (save in their closes)
> Than are lilies or roses :
> Like him that taught the woods sound Amaryllis.
> Goldings : you that have too too dainty Noses,
> Avaunt, go feed you them elsewhere on Roses.

On the 11th of November 1598 Dowland was engaged as an instrumentalist at the Danish court at a salary of 500 daler a year.

The King of Denmark, Christian IV, took a very lively interest in music, and was evidently willing to offer an almost unheard-of rate of pay in order to secure Dowland's services. In 1600 Dowland was granted, in addition to his salary, a further sum of 600 dalers, and in 1601 he received a decoration and a portrait of King Christian. In the following year he was sent to England to purchase musical instruments—and it is a pleasant, though entirely unsubstantiated, supposition that he may, in the course of this visit, have encountered Shakespeare, who was working on *Hamlet* at this time, and described to him the locality of Elsinore.

Dowland seems to have paid another visit to England some two years later and, like Handel, to have incurred the displeasure of his royal patron by too prolonged an absence. He remained altogether eight years in the service of the King of Denmark, and Angul Hammerich, in his *Musiken ved Christian den Fjerdes Hof* (1892), gives the following account of the circumstances which led to his dismissal :

' That there was some dissatisfaction with him can be seen from the Register of accounts for the years 1604–5 where, against the record that he was paid his full salary of 500 D., is entered the comment " although he has been in England on private business and overstayed the leave of absence granted him by the King ". Previous entries in the Register only hint at this absence. It also seems that he was in financial difficulties as well. On several occasions he drew his pay in advance, and an attempt to help him by placing one of the choir-boys of the Chapel under him as a lute pupil proved unavailing. His time was up. He had notice of dismissal on February 24. 1606 while the King was on a journey to Brunswick, and his departure left the accounts as to his salary in a state of great confusion.'

King Christian was evidently perturbed at the loss of so admirable a musician, in spite of the irregularities of his behaviour ; and little more than a year after Dowland had left his service, he applied to his sister Anne, the wife of King James I, for another English lutenist. The Queen, together with her son, Prince Henry, thereupon begged Lady Arabella Stuart to give up her lutenist, Thomas Cutting, who was a very celebrated performer and a composer as well, to the King of Denmark. So Cutting succeeded Dowland at the Danish court, and remained there four years. The correspondence between Prince Henry and Lady Arabella on this subject is preserved in the British Museum (Harleian MS. 6986).

In the meanwhile three further works of Dowland had been published in London during his absence in King Christian's service. First :

' The Second Booke of Songs or Ayres of 2. 4. and 5. parts : With Tableture for the Lute or Orpherian, with the Violl de Gamba. Composed by Iohn Dowland Batcheler of Musick and Lutenist to the King of Denmark : Also an excelent lesson for the Lute and Base Viol, called Dowlands adew. Published by George Eastland, and are to be sould at his house near the greene Dragon and Sword, in Fleetstreete. London : Printed by Thomas Este, the assigne of Thomas Morley. 1600.'

Dowland's dedication of the book to Lucy Countess of Bedford is dated ' From Helsingnoure (i. e. Elsinore) in Denmarke the first of Iune. 1600.' There is an additional dedication of the book by the publisher to the same lady, in the form of an acrostic on her name, and an address ' To the courteous reader ', in which Eastland extols the virtues of the book which he is offering to the public :

' Gentlemen : if the consideration of mine own estate or the true worth of money had prevailed with me, above the desire of pleasuring you and showing my love to my friend, this second labours of Maister Dowland (whose very name is a large preface of commendations to the book) had for ever lain hid in darkness, or at the least frozen in a cold and foreign country. I assure you that both my charge and pains in publishing it hath exceeded ordinary, yet thus much I have to assure me of requital, that neither the work is ordinary nor are your judgments ordinary to whom I present it : so that I have no reason but to hope for good increase in my labours, especially of your good favours toward me, which of all things I most esteem. Which I find in this, I mean shortly (God willing) to set at liberty for your service a prisoner taken at *Cales*, who if he discovers not something (in matter of music) worthy your knowledge, let the reputation of my judgement in music answer it. In the mean time, I commend my absent friend to your remembrance and my self to your favourable conceits.

GEORGE EASTLAND.'

The identity of the ' prisoner taken at Cadiz ' to whom East-land refers is unknown.

In this book Dowland's most celebrated composition, ' Lachri-mae ', or ' Flow, my tears ', makes its first appearance in print. That it was actually composed much earlier than 1600 is shown by its inclusion in William Ballet's manuscript collection of lute music (now preserved in the library of Trinity College, Dublin), which is dated 1594. This tune, which is in the form of a pavan, attained an extraordinary degree of popularity in the early years of the seventeenth century, both as a song and as an instrumental piece. The familiar way in which it is mentioned by the drama-tists of the period proves that it was quite a household word to the average member of the theatre audience for many years.

Now thou playest Dowland's *Lachrymae* to thy master.
(Thomas Middleton, *No Wit, no Help like a Woman* [1613].)
No, the man
In the moon dance a coranto, his bush
At 's back a-fire ; and his dog piping *Lachrymae*.
(Ben Jonson, *Time Vindicated* [1624].)
Arion, like a dolphin, playing *Lachrymae*.
(John Fletcher, *The Bloody Brother* [*c*. 1617].)
Wife. The fiddlers go again, husband.
Citizen. Ay, Nell ; but this is scurvy music. I gave the

C 2

whoreson gallows money, and I think he has not got me the
waits of Southwark : if I hear 'em not anon, I'll twinge him by
the ears.—You musicians, play *Baloo*!
Wife. No, good George, let 's ha' *Lachrymae*!

(Beaumont and Fletcher, *The Knight of the Burning Pestle*
[1611].)

Or with the hilts, thunder about your ears
Such music as will make your worships dance
To the doleful tune of *Lachrymae*.

(Philip Massinger, *The Maid of Honour* [1621].)

Is your Theorbo
Turn'd to a distaff, Signior ? and your voice
With which you chanted *Room for a lusty Gallant*
Tun'd to the note of *Lachrymae* ?)

(Philip Massinger, *The Picture* [1629].)

You'll be made dance *Lachrymae*, I fear, at the cart's tail.

(John Webster, *The Devil's Law Case* [1623].)

The Fitzwilliam Virginal Book contains two acknowledged
arrangements of the *Lachrymae* for the virginals, one by William
Byrd and one by Giles Farnaby. But the very beautiful Pavan
by Thomas Morley, which has been described by the modern
editors of the Fitzwilliam Book and by such commentators on it
as Charles Van Den Borren, E. W. Naylor, Granville Bantock,
and E. H. Fellowes as Morley's setting of Dowland's *Lachrymae*
(though there is no authority for such an ascription in the manuscript), is an original work of Morley's that bears but a chance
resemblance to the *Lachrymae* in the opening phrase. It does,
however, bear a remarkable likeness to an acknowledged Pavan
of Morley's in Robert Dowland's *Varietie of Lute Lessons*.

Dowland's 'Third And Last Booke Of Songs Or Aires. Newly
composed to sing to the Lute, Orpharion, or viols, and a dialogue
for a base and meane Lute with five voices to sing thereto. 1603 '
was not, in point of fact, his last book of songs. It was dedicated

to [Sir] 'John Souch, Esquire', and opens with the following 'Epistle to the Reader':

'The applause of them that judge is the encouragement of those that write. My first two books of ayres speed so well that they have produced a third which they have fetched far from home and brought even through the most perilous seas, where having escaped so many sharp rocks, I hope they shall not be wrecked on land by curious and biting censures. As in a hive of bees all labour alike to lay up honey, opposing themselves against none but fruitless drones, so in the house of learning and fame, all good endeavourers should strive to add somewhat that is good, not malicing one another, but altogether bandying against the idle and malicious ignorant. My labours for my part I freely offer to every man's judgment, presuming that favour once attained is more easily increased than lost. JOHN DOWLAND.'

It will be observed that whereas the songs in the first book were designed to be sung to the accompaniment of the lute *or* bass viol, those of the second book are set for the lute *with* the bass viol, while the title of the third book suggests the possible substitution of viols for some of the voices. The question of the instruments employed for the accompaniment of the ayres in general will be discussed in a later chapter.

In 1605 appeared Dowland's only publication for instruments without the addition of voices. This was:

'Lachrimae Or Seaven Teares figured in seaven passionate Pavans, with divers other Pavans, Galiards, and Almands, set forth for the Lute, Viols, or Violons, in five parts: By Iohn Dowland Bacheler of Musicke, and Lutenist to the most Royall and Magnificent Christian the fourth, King of Denmarke, Norway, Vandales, and Gothes, Duke of Sleswicke, Holsten, Stormaria, and Ditmarsh: Earle of Oldenburge and Delmenhorst.

Aut Furit, aut Lachrimat, quem non Fortuna beavit.

London. Printed by Iohn Windet, dwelling at the Signe of the Crosse Keyes at Powles Wharfe, and are to be solde at the Authors house in Fetter lane neare Fleete streete.' 1605.

The book is dedicated ' To the Most Gracious and Sacred Princesse Anna Queene of England, Scotland, France and Ireland ' in these words :

' Since I had access to your Highness at Winchester (most gracious Queen) I have been twice under sail for Denmark, hastening my return to my most royal King and Master, your dear and worthiest brother ; but by contrary winds and frost I was forced back again, and of necessity compelled to winter here in your most happy kingdom. In which time I have endeavoured by my poor labour and study to manifest my humbleness and duty to your highness, being myself one of your most affectionate subjects, and also servant to your most princely brother, the only patron and sun-shine of my else unhappy fortunes. For which respects I have presumed to dedicate this work of music to your sacred hands, that was begun where you were born, and ended where you reign. And though the title doth promise tears, unfit guests in these joyful times, yet no doubt pleasant are the tears which music weeps, neither are tears shed always in sorrow, but sometime in joy and gladness. Vouchsafe then (worthy goddess) your gracious protection to these showers of harmony, lest if you frown on them they be metamorphosed into true tears.

Your Majesty's in all humility devoted
JOHN DOWLAND.'

To the reader he says :

' Having in foreign parts met divers lute lessons of my composition published by strangers without my name or approbation, I thought it much more convenient that my labours should pass forth under mine own allowance, receiving from me their last foil and polishment ; for which consideration I have undergone this long and troublesome work, wherein I have mixed new songs with old, grave with light, that every ear may receive his several content. . . .'

The ' seven passionate pavans ' of the title are called severally *Lachrimae Antiquae, Lachrimae Antiquae Novae, Lachrimae Gementes, Lachrimae Tristes, Lachrimae Coactae, Lachrimae Amantis,* and *Lachrimae Verae.* The first is almost identical with the song, ' Flow, my tears ', in the second book of ayres; the others all derive thematically from the first, and if it cannot be said that they go very far in the direction of illustrating the different adjectives bestowed on them, they certainly contain some of the most finished and beautiful instrumental music of their period. A pendant to the seven passionate pavans is entitled *Semper Dowland semper Dolens*, and this is followed by ' Sir Henry Umpton's Funeral ', ' M. John Langton's Pavan ', ' The King of Denmark's Galliard ', and eight other galliards, each inscribed to a separate gentleman. Among these is ' Captain Piper's Galliard ', which had already figured in the first book of ayres as a song, to the words ' If my complaints could passions move '. The volume concludes with a couple of sprightly Almands, by way of contrast to the gravity of the preceding numbers.

Dowland's next publication was the translation of Andreas Ornithoparcus's immense treatise on music called *Micrologus*, which was printed originally at Leipzig in 1517. Dowland's conservatism in all matters relating to the theory of music conflicts somewhat strangely with the pioneering spirit revealed in all his creative work. In introducing his translation of this century-old work to the English reader, he asserts that ' there is no writer more worthy in the art of music than this author Ornithoparcus ', in spite of the fact that his own countryman, Thomas Morley's admirable treatise had already been on the market for twelve years when he issued the *Micrologus* in translation.

The book is quite medieval in its outlook on music, and makes very stiff reading for the present-day student, despite the pleasantness of Dowland's prose style. There are, however, entertaining episodes such as the section headed :

Who be called Singers

' The practitioner of this faculty is called a Cantor, who doth pronounce and sing those things which the musician by a rule of reason doth set down; so that the harmony is nothing worth if the Cantor seek to utter it without the rules of reason, and unless he comprehend that which he pronounceth in the purity of his understanding. Therefore well saith Ioan. Papa. 22. cap. 2. To whom shall I compare a Cantor better than to a drunkard, which indeed goeth home, but by which path he cannot tell. A musician to a Cantor is as a Praetor to a cryer, which is proved by this sentence of Guido:

> Twixt musicians and practitians odds is great;
> They do know, these but show, what art doth treat.
> Who doeth aught, yet knoweth naught, is brute by kind.
> If voices shrill, void of skill, may honour find,
> Then Philomel must bear the bell,
> And Balaam's ass musician was.

Therefore a speculative musician excels the practick: for it is much better to know what a man doth than to do that which another man doth. Hence it is that buildings and triumphs are attributed to them who had the command and rule, not to them by whose work and labour they were performed. Therefore there is great difference in calling one a musician, or a Cantor. For Quintilian saith: That musicians were so honoured amongst men famous for wisdom that the same men were accounted musicians and prophets, and wise men; but Guido compareth those Cantors (which have made courtesy afar off to music) to brute beasts.'

Of 'Ten precepts necessary for every singer', the ninth is:

'The uncomely gaping of the mouth, and ungraceful motion of the body is a sign of a mad singer.'

These precepts are preceded by some amusing remarks on 'The divers fashions of singing':

'Every man lives after his own humour, neither are all men governed by the same laws; and divers nations have divers fashions, and differ in habit, diet, studies, speech, and song. Hence is it that the English do carol, the French sing, the Spaniards weep, the Italians which dwell about the coasts of Ianua caper with their voices, the other bark; but the Germans (which I am ashamed to utter) do howl like wolves.'

But one would gladly sacrifice the whole of this ponderous and pedantic tome in exchange for one single addition to the number of Dowland's songs.

Passing over the three ayres contributed by Dowland to his son Robert's *Musicall Banquet* (which will be referred to later), and the *Observations belonging to Lute-playing*, which are of purely technical interest (apart from the remark : ' Myself was born but 30 years after Hans Gerle's book was printed,' and Robert's description of his father as ' being now grey, and, like the swan, but singing towards his end '), we come to Dowland's last, and in many respects best publication :

' A Pilgrimes Solace. Wherein is contained Musicall Harmonie of 3. 4. and 5. parts, to be sung and plaid with the Lute and Viols. 1612.'

On the title-page Dowland describes himself as ' Lutenist to the Right Honourable the Lord Walden ' (son of the Earl of Suffolk), to whom the book is dedicated.

The address to the reader is a document of very great interest, and touches on several points which require some elucidation :

' Worthy Gentlemen, and my loving countrymen : moved by your many and fore-tasted courtesies, I am constrained to appear again unto you. True it is, I have lien long obscured from your sight, because I received a kingly entertainment in a foreign climate, which could not attain to any (though never so mean) place at home ; yet have I held up my head within this horizon, and not altogether been unaffected else where, since some part of my poor labours have found favour in the greatest part of Europes, and been printed in eight most famous cities beyond the seas, viz: Paris, Antwerpe, Collein, Nurenburge, Franckfort, Liepsig, Amsterdam, and Hamburge (yea, and some of them also authorized under the Emperor's privilege). Yet I must tell you, as I have been a stranger, so have I again found strange entertainment since my return, especially by the opposition of two sorts of people that shroud themselves under the title of musicians. The first are some simple Cantors, or vocal singers, who though they seem excellent in their blind division-making, are merely ignorant, even in the first elements of music, and also in the true order of the mutation of the Hexachord in the System, (which hath been approved by all the learned and skilful men of Christendom this 800 years); yet do these fellows give their verdict of me behind my back, and say what I do is after the old manner. But I will speak openly to them, and would have them know that the proudest Cantor of them dares not oppose himself face to face against me. The second are young men, professors of the lute, who vaunt themselves, to the disparagement of such as have been before their time, (wherein I myself am a party) that there never was the like of them. To these men I say little because of my love and hope to see some deeds ensue their brave words, and also being that here under their own noses hath been published a book in defence of the Viol de Gamba, wherein not only all other the best and principal instruments have been abased, but especially the lute by name. The words, to satisfy thee, Reader, I have here thought good to insert, and are as followeth : *From henceforth the stateful instrument Gambo Viol shall with ease yield full various and deviceful music as the lute ; for here I protest the Trinity of Music—Parts, Passion and Division —to be as gracefully united in the Gambo Viol as in the most received instrument that is.* Which imputation, methinks, the learneder sort of musician ought not to let pass unanswered. Moreover that here are and daily doth come into our most famous kingdom divers strangers from beyond the seas, which aver before our own faces that we have no true method of application or fingering of the lute. Now if these gallant young lutenists be such as they would have the world believe and of which I make no doubt, let them remember that their skill lieth not in their fingers ends : *Cucullus non facit monachum.* I wish for the honour, therefore, and general benefit of our country that they undertake the defence of their lute profession, seeing that some of them above other have most large means, convenient time, and such encouragement as I never knew any have. Believe me, if any of these objections had been made when those famous men lived which now are thought worthy of no fame, not derogating from these skilful men present, I dare affirm that these objections had been answered to the full ; and I make no doubt but that those few of the former time which live yet, being that some of them are Bachelors of Music and others which assume unto themselves to be no less worthy, will be as forward to preserve their reputation. Perhaps you will ask me why I that have travelled many countries and ought to have some experience, doth not undergo this business myself? I answer that I want ability, being I am now entered into the fiftieth year of mine age : secondly because I want both means, leisure and encouragement. But (Gentle Reader, to conclude, although abruptly) this work of mine which I here have published containeth such things as I myself have thought well of, as being in mine opinion furnished with variety of matter both of judgment and delight ; which willingly I refer to the friendly censure and approbation of the skilful, hoping it will be no less delightful to all in general than it was pleasing to me in the composition.

Farewell
Your friend
JOHN DOULAND.'

It is not unlikely that when Dowland ' had 'access ' to Queen Anne at Winchester (in September or October 1603) he may have tried to solicit her influence to secure a position as lutenist at the court of King James. But the Queen was probably unwilling to take any action that would deprive her brother, King Christian, of a much-valued servant, and after Dowland's somewhat ignominious dismissal from the Danish court it was obviously out of the question that he should be immediately taken into the royal service in England, more especially as the King of Denmark came to England to visit King James I in the summer of 1606. However, soon after the publication of *A Pilgrimes Solace*, Dowland attained the position he had so long desired, being appointed one of the King's musicians for the lutes in October 1612, at a salary of 20 pence a day,[1] with an allowance of £16 2s. 6d. per annum for livery. In 1618 his name appears in the Audit Office Accounts as second musician for the lutes, Robert Johnson being the first, but in the accounts for 1624 his name precedes Johnson's.

---

[1] The value of money was then about ten times as much as it is now.

No complete book of Dowland's work is known to have been printed on the Continent, but a good deal of his lute-music found its way into foreign publications such as Rude's *Flores musicae* (1600), Füllsack's *Auserlesener Paduanen* (1602), and Van der Hove's *Delitiae Musicae* (1612).

No modern student of the music of *A Pilgrimes Solace* would agree with the verdict of the 'simple Cantors' who considered Dowland's work to be 'after the old manner'; indeed this book contains some of the most astonishingly advanced and original songs of the period. The 'simple Cantors' were probably of much the same mentality as the operatic singers of the last century (and many 'simple Cantors' of this); they objected to Dowland because he wrote music for its own sake and not for theirs. Florid vocal passages, which were just coming into vógue in England in the second decade of the seventeenth century, are conspicuous by their absence in Dowland's music; but this is the only element of novelty that is not to be found in the songs of *A Pilgrimes Solace*.

The 'book in defence of the Viol de Gamba' was Captain Tobias Hume's *Musicall Humours*, and the preface quoted by Dowland will be given in full in the chapter devoted to that composer.

It appears that by 1612 Dowland had abandoned his former intention of writing a treatise on lute-playing; but he was evidently at work on a book of this kind but two years previously, for his son Robert, introducing his *Varietie of Lute-lessons* to the public in 1610, says that this work may serve its purpose 'until my father hath finished his greater work touching the art of Lute-playing'.

Of the last fourteen years of Dowland's life practically nothing is known. In 1612 Henry Peacham published in his *Minerva Britannica* a poem (reproduced herewith) alluding to England's neglect of Dowland in his old age, and this reproach may possibly

Ad amicum ſuum Iohannem Doulandum Muſices peritiſſimum.

Iohannes Doulandus.

Annos ludendo hauſi.

H EERE *Philomel*, in ſilence ſits alone,
In depth of winter, on the bared brier,
Whereas the Roſe, had once her beautie ſhowen;
Which Lordes, and Ladies, did ſo much deſire:
But fruitles now, in winters froſt, and ſnow,
It doth deſpiſ'd, and vnregarded grow,

So ſince (old frend,) thy yeares haue made thee white,
And thou for others, haſt conſum'd thy ſpring,
How few regard thee, whome thou didſt delight,
And farre, and neere, came once to heare thee ſing:
Ingratefull times, and worthles age of ours,
That let's vs pine, when it hath cropt our flowers.

M 1.   *Cui*

A page from Henry Peacham's *Minerva Britannica*.

have helped to secure his appointment as court musician later in the same year. The marginal note to the poem in *Minerva Britannica* (Anagramma Authoris) seems to show that the oft-quoted anagram :

JOHANNES   DOULANDUS
ANNOS LUDENDO HAUSI

was made by Peacham, and not, as Fuller says in his *Worthies of England* (1662), ' by Ralph Sadler Esq. of Standon in Hertford-shire, who was with him at Copenhagen '. Fuller's account of Dowland is manifestly inaccurate on many points of known fact, and this leads one to attach but little importance to his assertion that Dowland was born in the city of Westminster, but his estimate of Dowland as man and musician is worth quoting :

' He was the rarest musician that his age did behold ; having travelled beyond the seas, and compounded English with foreign skill in that faculty, it is questionable whether he excelled in vocal or instrumental music.   A cheerful person he was, passing his days in lawful merriment, truly answering the anagram made of him.'

The Audit Office Accounts show that Dowland received his salary as court musician for ' one quarter of a year ended at Christmas 1625 and xxvi days in part of other Lady Day quarter, 1626 ', and his son Robert, who succeeded him in his position at court, was paid at Michaelmas 1626, ' from the death of his said father ' ; so it may reasonably be concluded that John Dowland died on the 21st of January 1626.

One is bestowing no careless or exaggerated praise on Dowland in asserting that among his seventy part-songs and eighteen songs for solo voice and lute there is not a single bad or uninteresting piece of work ; in fact, this negative statement rather underrates the quality of his songs than overrates them, they are all so good. Compared with that of Schubert and some other modern song-writers, Dowland's output is not large ; but against this we must set his astonishing versatility in the expression of so many widely different moods, and the fact that he seldom, if ever, repeats himself: every song has its own quite definite individuality. In the first book we find simple metrical tunes quite simply harmonized in four parts (such as the well-known ' Awake, sweet love ', ' Now, O now I needs must part ', and ' Away with these self-loving lads '), side by side with deeply expressive serious songs laid out on big lines, with a good deal of independence in the movement of the inner parts (as ' Come, heavy sleep ', and ' All ye whom Love or Fortune hath betrayed ', and ' Burst forth, my tears ', which were obviously conceived as part-songs and only provided with a lute-part as a makeshift substitute for such voices as might not on occasion be at hand) ; and then there are those delicious, light-footed ayres, so subtle in the interplay of their rhythms for all that they run so trippingly on the tongue : ' Come away, come, sweet love ', and ' Can she excuse my wrongs with Virtue's cloak ', a type of song we meet with several times again in the third book and, in a more extended form, in *A Pilgrimes Solace*, from which ' Shall I strive with words to move ' and ' Were every thought an eye ' may be cited as excellent examples. Several of the songs in the first book were, we learn from the preface, composed many years before they were published—in this connexion it is interesting to speculate as to whether the *airs de cour* and *chansons dansées* which Dowland must have heard during his sojourn in France in 1580–2 exercised any influence in determining the form in which his compositions were cast. It is, at any rate, significant that Charles Tessier's *Premier livre de chansons et airs de cour* was published in London in the same year as Dowland's first book of ayres.

The second book of songs shows increased power in the handling of words expressive of sorrow and despair. Dowland never excelled, though he may have equalled, the profoundly beautiful song with which the book begins, ' I saw my lady weep ' (dedicated ' To the most famous Anthony Holborne '), from which a passage may be quoted to illustrate the wonderful wealth of harmonic resource which he had at his disposal.

Example 5.

Her face was full of woe, full . . of woe, But

. . such a woe (be-lieve me) as wins more hearts Than

The famous 'Lachrimae' and 'Sorrow, stay' are two other notable songs of sadness in this book, and one cannot help wondering whether the song beginning

> Come, ye heavy states of night,
> Do my father's spirit right,

may not have a more than fortuitous connexion with 'Helsingnoure in Denmarke'.

One of Dowland's finest songs, 'In darkness let me dwell', is to be found, with two others which do not appear in any of the other books, in his son's *Musical Banquet*. This is a fitting companion to 'Lachrimae' and 'I saw my lady weep', and one of the great songs of English music. After a few bars of instrumental prelude, the voice enters with this noble phrase :

Example 6.

The atmosphere of tragic gloom is maintained throughout the song. An impassioned outburst :

Example 7.

let me liv-ing, let me liv - ing, liv-ing die,

leads to a remarkable antiphonal passage between the lute and the bass viol which is almost unique in the song-books, since as a general rule the viol merely doubles the bass notes of the lute part ; and a thrilling effect is obtained at the close of the song by the whispered repetition of the opening phrase—another touch of unique originality.

Yet another aspect of Dowland's many-sided nature is revealed in the exquisite delicacy and tenderness of the two fountain songs in the third book. But taken as a whole, *A Pilgrimes Solace* must be regarded as his masterpiece, and the crown of his life's achievement. In every number in this amazing book we see his genius displayed in its full maturity. It is a remarkable fact that this book, appearing at a time when the polyphonic tradition was fast giving way before the figured bass and its attendant harmonic developments, is at once the most contrapuntal of Dowland's works, and the one in which the widest range of purely harmonic combinations may be found. This was indeed ' new music ', but it bore little resemblance to the ' new music ' of the Italians, who were bent on making music subservient to diction. Careful as he was in setting words with just note and accent (in spite of some accentual misfits in the second and third verses of certain songs—an accident almost inseparable from the strophic form which repeats the same music for every verse),

Dowland was not the man to sacrifice any element of musical expression to merely verbal exigences ; and in one or two of the songs in *A Pilgrimes Solace* the rhythmic flexibility of the inner parts necessitates a good deal of juggling with the words, as in the following example :

Example 8.

O . . . that   time's strange time's strange ef-fects, ef-fects

Two very fine songs in this book are provided with an obbligato for the treble viol, in addition to the usual accompaniment for the lute and bass viol (it may, incidentally, be mentioned here that the bass strings of the pianoforte, and even of the harpsichord, give out far more tone than did those of the lute, which, without the addition of the bass viol, would provide a rather inadequate support to the voice ; it is therefore a mistake to add the tone of a violoncello to that of the pianoforte in a modern rendering of these songs, for the bass line then outweighs the rest of the harmony).

But it is less than just to select for special mention some few songs from so large a number of good things ; one has no sooner referred by name to one than another of equal excellence suggests itself. Of all the song-writers Dowland was indeed ' the rarest musician that his age did behold '. He chose for musical setting some of the most perfect lyrics that have ever been written in the English language, yet never did he fail to re-create the full beauty of the poet's thought in music; and though Byrd and others of his contemporaries excelled in larger forms of composition, no one has left us a musical legacy of more intrinsic loveliness than John Dowland.

122914

3

John Danyel

WHEN Thomas Tomkins published his Songs of 3. 4. 5. and 6.
parts in 1622, he dedicated each madrigal in the set to a separate
person—some to his relations, others to various eminent musicians
of his day. Thus William Byrd, Orlando Gibbons, John Ward,
Thomas Warrock, and others receive a madrigal apiece. Was it,
then, with intent of subtle homage that Tomkins divided the two
sections of a single madrigal between ' Doctor Douland ' and
' Master John Daniell ', as though he would name them together
as the two greatest living masters of accompanied song among
his fellow-countrymen? The supposition is not altogether
fanciful, and it is just possible that the opening phrase of the
madrigal in question, as well as certain phrases in Danyel's song,
' Eyes, look no more ', are deliberate quotations from Dowland's
most famous work, ' Lachrimae '—although, it must be admitted,
musical quotations were rarely met with at this time, and the
phrase is by no means an uncommon occurrence in the works of
composers who knew nothing of Dowland's song.

John Danyel is at present almost completely unknown; his
genius has certainly not received anything like adequate recognition from the historians of music, who for the most part ignore
him altogether. The British Museum possesses the sole surviving
copy of his only published work—a book containing eighteen
songs for a solo voice accompanied by lute and bass viol, one song
for four voices (the unusual combination of S.S.A.T.) and lute,
one song for four voices and two lutes, and one lute solo (a set of
variations on a tune also treated by William Byrd (for viols) and
William Inglott (for virginals) and here quaintly entitled ' Mrs.
Anne Grene her leaves be greene ', in honour of the book's dedi-
catee), and that is all we have of Danyel's compositions. Of his

life we know next to nothing. There is no account of him in Grove's Dictionary of Music. But as a composer of serious songs in extended form he stands second only to John Dowland among the composers of the great period of English song; and for the bold originality of his harmonic sense, which is always controlled by a polished technique and a sure instinct for beauty of sound, and, too, for the breadth and spaciousness of his style, so widely different from the almost miniature song-forms of Rosseter, Campion, and others, Danyel deserves an honourable place in musical history.

He was brother to Samuel Danyel the poet—probably a younger brother. Fuller, in his *Worthies*, says that Samuel Danyel was the son of a John Danyel whom he describes as a ' music-master ', adding that ' his harmonious mind made an impression on his son's genius, who proved an exquisite poet '. But nothing is known of the father, and Grosart in his ' Memorial-Introduction ' to Samuel Danyel's complete works suggests that Fuller may have confused the musical brother John with the supposed father. According to Fuller, Samuel Danyel was born in 1562, ' not far from Taunton, Somersetshire '. We do not know the date and place of John Danyel's birth. He took his Mus.Bac. degree at Christ Church, Oxford, in July 1604, and in 1606 he published his book of *Songs for the Lute, Viol, and Voice*, ' at the Signe of the White Lyon, Paules Church Yard '.

The book is prefaced with an interesting dedication—the only verse dedication, save of Campion's, to be found in the English song-books of the period :

To Mistress Anne Grene, the worthy Daughter of Sir William Grene of Milton, Knight

That which was only privately compos'd
For your delight, fair ornament of worth,
Is here come to be publicly disclos'd
And to an universal view put forth,

Which having been but yours and mine before
(Or but of few besides) is made hereby
To be the world's, and yours and mine no more.
So that in this sort giving it to you
I give it from you and therein do wrong
To make that which in private was your due
Thus to the world in common to belong,
And thereby may debase the estimate
Of what perhaps did bear some price before.
For oft we see how things of slender rate,
Being undivulg'd, are choicely held in store,
And rarer compositions once expos'd
Are (as unworthy of the world) condemn'd:
For what, but by their having been disclos'd
To all, hath made all mysteries contemn'd?
And therefore why had it not been enow
That Milton only heard our melody?
Where Baucis and Philemon only show
To Gods and men their hospitality
And thereunto a joyful ear afford
In midst of their well welcom'd company
Where we (as birds do to themselves record)
Might entertain our private harmony.
But fearing lest that time might have beguil'd
You of your own and me of what was mine,
I did desire to have it known my Child
And for his right, to others I resign.
Though I might have been warn'd by him, who is
Both near and dear to me, that what we give
Unto these times, we give t' unthankfulness,
And so without unconstant censures live.
　　　But yet these humours will no warning take,
　　　We still must blame the fortune that we make.
And yet herein we do adventure now
But Ayre for Ayre, no danger can accrue;
They are but our refusals we bestow,
And we thus cast the old t' have room for new,
Which I must still address t' your learned hand
Who me and all I am shall still command.

JOHN DANYEL.

The Milton where Danyel stayed was the little hamlet of Milton Clevedon, between Shepton Mallet and Bruton, in Somersetshire. This dedication is so different in tone from the conventional panegyrics usually addressed by the composers of the time to their patrons, that one is inclined to think of Danyel rather as a friend of the Grene family than as a musician employed in their service ; and, indeed, Anthony à Wood, in his *Athenae Oxonienses*, says that Samuel Danyel came of a wealthy family. But on this point there is no certain evidence.

John Danyel seems to have shared his poet-brother's modesty and reluctance to publish his work. Samuel Danyel's first publication—the famous ' Delia ' sonnets—was practically forced upon him by the surreptitious inclusion of twenty-seven of his sonnets in Newman and Nashe's pirated edition of Sir Philip Sidney's *Astrophel and Stella* (1591). In dedicating his own edition of the sonnets to the Countess of Pembroke (' Sidney's sister, Pembroke's mother '), in 1592, Samuel Danyel wrote :

' Although I rather desired to keep in the private passions of my youth from the multitude, as things uttered to myself and consecrated to silence ; yet seeing I was betrayed by the indiscretion of a greedy printer, and had some of my secrets bewrayed to the world uncorrected, doubting the like of the rest, I am forced to publish that which I never meant. But this wrong was not only done to me, but to him whose unmatchable lines have endured the like misfortune, Ignorance sparing not to commit sacrilege upon so holy reliques. . . . For myself, seeing I am thrust out into the world, and that my unboldened Muse is forced to appear so rawly in public, I desire only to be graced by the countenance of your protection, whom the fortune of our time hath made the happy and judicial Patroness of the Muses (a glory hereditary to your house), to preserve them from those hideous Beasts, Oblivion and Barbarism.'

And again, in the preface to *Tethys' Festival ; or, The Queen's Wake* (1610), he writes in the same vein :

' I thank God I labour not with that disease of ostentation, nor affect to be known to be the man, *digitoque monstrarier hic est,* having my name already wider in this kind than I desire, and more in the wind than I would.'

In 1618 John Danyel succeeded his brother as censor to all plays performed by the Children of the Queen's Revels, a company of youthful actors with which two other composers, Philip Rosseter and Robert Jones, had been associated some years previously, and in the following year the poet died at Beckington, in Somersetshire, where he lies buried, having appointed his 'faithful brother' John his sole executor. Four years later John Danyel published an edition of his brother's poetical works, with an epistle dedicatory 'To the High and most Illustrious Prince CHARLES His Excellence' (afterwards King Charles I), which opens thus :

' SIR : Presents to gods were offered by the hands of Graces ; and why not those of great Princes by those of the Muses ? To you, therefore, Great Prince of Honour and Honour of Princes, I jointly present Poesy and Music ; in the one the service of my defunct Brother, in the other the duty of myself living, in both the devotion of two Brothers, your Highness' humble servants.'

In 1625 John Danyel is mentioned as being a member of the royal company of the musicians for the lutes and voices. And that is all we know of him, except his music.

Though Danyel chiefly excelled as a composer of serious songs built on a large scale, his half-dozen shorter songs in lighter vein are equally individual and full of beauty, particularly ' Why canst thou not as others do ', ' Thou pretty bird ', and ' I die whenas I do not see her ', with its curious anticipation of ' The Vicar of Bray '. They have not the merry, light-hearted gaiety of Jones and Campion—their texts would scarcely warrant it— but there is in them a strength of line and a firmness of structure that are all Danyel's own. Unlike many songs of the period, they are all-of-a-piece from start to finish ; the melodic outline is sustained throughout the song, and is not a mere sequence of short phrases.

Of the serious songs, the most important are the two cycles of three songs—or perhaps one should rather call them songs in three movements. The first bears the title, ' Mrs. M. E., her Funerall teares for the death of her husband ', and is a work of poignant and sustained beauty ; the second, which is the more remarkable of the two, has been recently published under the title of ' Chromatic Tunes ', though it bears no special title in the original song-book. The text runs as follows :

Can doleful notes to measur'd accents set
Express unmeasur'd griefs which time forget ?
No, let chromatic tunes, harsh without ground,
Be sullen music for a tuneless heart.
Chromatic tunes most like my passions sound,
As if combin'd to bear their falling part.
Uncertain certain turns, of thoughts forecast,
Bring back the same, then die and dying last.

The rise and development of chromaticism in English music is a rather mysterious subject. Musical historians have accustomed us to associate chromaticism in the music of the Renaissance with the Italians, Cipriano de Rore, Luca Marenzio, and—most daring and original of all—Gesualdo, Prince of Venosa. But the chromaticism of the latter is largely homophonic, and, moreover, the madrigals in which the most remarkable examples of it occur did not appear in print until 1611, although they were actually written some years earlier. How, then, are we to account for the appearance in England, as early as 1597–8, of two such works as Weelkes's three-part madrigal. ' Cease sorrows now ' and Giles Farnaby's four-part canzonet, ' Consture my meaning ', in which a fully developed sense of chromatic harmony is interwoven into the polyphonic tissue with such consummate mastery that it is evident that, so far from being experiments in a strange idiom, these works, together with Danyel's 'Chromatic Tunes' of 1606, are but the culmination of a train of musical thought which must have been occupying composers' minds for many years previously? It is, of course, easy to show that much earlier in the sixteenth century English musicians of the strict contrapuntal school admitted into their compositions far stranger combinations of sounds than did their Italian contemporaries, but there is a very wide difference between the rare and comparatively mild chromaticism to be found in the works of Byrd and his predecessors, and the chromaticism of Weelkes and Farnaby and Danyel in the works referred to above.

The 'Chromatic Tunes' cycle is constructed on such big lines, and each section is so homogeneous and closely knit, that it is difficult to convey any adequate impression of its unique style by means of short quotations. The first part, comprising the first couplet of the poem, is evolved from a subject which is treated fugally :

Example 9.

and the words ' unmeasur'd griefs which time forget ' are treated in a wonderfully expressive manner :

Example 10.

The second part opens with a phrase of a kind which, familiar
though it became in the time of Purcell, must have sounded
strange indeed to the amateurs of 1606:

Example 11.

tunes,   no,   let chro - ma - tic   tunes

Another characteristic of Danyel is his admirable use of pedal-points, as at :

Be   sul - len mu - sic for   a   tune - less heart

and again at the end of the second part :

Example 13.

As   if . . com - bin'd   to bear

their fall - - ing part.

The third part of the song is less chromatic, but no less remarkable than the preceding sections, on account of its subtle rhythmic designs :

Example 14.

Bring back the same, then die, then die . . and dy - ing

last, then die, and dy - - ing, and dy - - ing last,

Another beautiful pedal-point brings to a quiet conclusion what is surely one of the finest songs ever written by an Englishman.

Of the single songs, the most interesting is the pavan-like 'Eyes, look no more', a grave and noble piece of work which strikes a fine note of sombre passion at its close :

Example 15.

In 1625 two books of lute-music (now lost) were published at Hanau by one Johann Daniel, under the title of *Thesaurus gratiarum, d. i. Schatzkästlein, darinnen allerhand Stücklein, Präambuln, Toccaden, Fugen etc. zur Lauten-Tabulatur gebracht, aus verschiedenen Autoribus.* But there is no evidence to persuade us that this was the work of our English lutenist, nor have I been able to find any lute-music by Danyel (except the rather doubtful 'Daniell's Jigge' in the University Library, Cambridge) in any of the English manuscript collections.

4

Robert Jones

OF all the song composers of this brilliant period no one has been more completely or more unaccountably neglected than Robert Jones, composer of ayres and madrigals, theatrical manager, and controversialist. With the exception of one or two duets which appeared in Mr. Kennedy Scott's *Euterpe* series, and a few hopeless travesties of his work printed by Rimbault and his untrustworthy like, none of Jones's songs were available in print until 1922. And yet there is no composer of the period whose work seems more likely to make an immediate appeal, not only to musicians, but even to the most unsophisticated music-lovers for whom historical considerations count for nothing. His style is admirably simple and direct, and his light-hearted gaiety, his lyrical gift of melody, and his real sense of humour in music fully entitle him to be regarded as the Sullivan of his day—though in certain other respects the comparison does not hold good.

This Robert Jones is, as Dr. Grattan Flood has pointed out in his book on *Early Tudor Composers*, quite a different person from his namesake, the pre-Reformation composer of church music, who was a Gentleman of the Chapel Royal in 1512. But it would seem that Dr. Grattan Flood is in error when he proceeds to say that the later Robert Jones was born about the year 1570. We learn from the preface to the latter's first book of songs that he had practised singing ever since he had practised speaking; and when he came to take his musical degree at Oxford in 1597 it was stated that he had studied music for sixteen years. We have therefore no reasonable ground for fixing the date of his birth any earlier than 1575 or 1576. Very little is known of his life, but his elaborate and vigorously written prefaces and dedicatory addresses in the song-books throw a good deal of light on his personality and upon the relation that existed in his time between the composer and the public.

We must not forget that in those days there were no public concerts and no professional critics. Music was heard in the church, in the home, and in the tavern, and every man was his own critic. But there was a musical profession—perhaps it would be more correct to say that there were two musical professions : the one secular, the other ecclesiastical ; and, as we have seen already, there were two traditions of music sharply opposed to one another, though the secular tradition, relying on oral methods for its persistence, has not been preserved for us by history. The result is that musical historians, ignoring the existence of a secular tradition, have greatly exaggerated the importance of what they are pleased to call the homophonic revolution at the end of the sixteenth century. There was, in point of fact, no revolution at all, only a gradual process of fusion between the two traditions, each imparting new strength and vitality to the other, and we see the process at work all through the golden period of English music. After 1625 began the period of decline and decadence, illuminated only by the moderate talents of the brothers Lawes and the solitary genius of Henry Purcell towards the end of the century ; polyphony decayed and the almost infinite resources of the modes were whittled down to the harmonic limitations of the two diatonic scales.

Now Jones was of the secular tradition, a descendant of the minstrel of the Middle Ages, whose music, enjoyed by the multitude of high and low degree, was no doubt viewed with contempt by the respectable professionals of the rival tradition— more especially as the medieval minstrel and, as we shall see from one of Jones's dedications, his later counterpart were looked upon as rather disreputable members of society. Hence the urgent necessity for patronage and regular employment either at Court or in the house of some rich nobleman.

The fact of his having taken a musical degree tends to show that Jones had a strong desire to be accounted a serious musician of the established order, but his genius led him in another direction, and utterly deserted him, as did also his technical compétence and his sense of humour, whenever he tried his hand at a work of grave and serious character : the result was almost always dull to the verge of the ridiculous. And whether we attribute it to his rather ludicrous achievements in this kind of music, or to his having neglected the larger forms and concentrated upon genial tunes and comic songs, the fact remains that he came in for a good deal of adverse and contemptuous criticism, to which, however, he lost no time and spared no pains in replying. But he had no exaggerated idea of his own capacity as a musician, for he admits in the preface to his *Ultimum Vale* that he is ' not ignorant enough to be grossly taxed by any of our cunning masters, nor big enough to be flattered or envied '.

His first work was published in 1600 under the title of *The First Booke of Songes and Ayres of foure parts with Tableture for the Lute. So made that all the parts together, or either of them severally may be song to the Lute, Orpherian or Viol de Gambo.* The wording, with its obscure second sentence, is precisely the same as that of the title of John Dowland's first book of songs, and is doubtless the work of the publisher, Peter Short, the assignee of Thomas Morley, who had at that time a monopoly for the printing of music-books. It was obviously not the composer's intention that the alto or tenor parts should be sung separately to the lute, orpherian, or viol de gambo, for the songs are true part-songs, that is to say, simply-harmonized tunes, having nothing in common with the polyphonic style of the madrigal. The ambiguous phrase was certainly meant to imply that if the three lower voices were absent the *tune* could be sung

E

just as well to the accompaniment of the lute, orpherian, or viol de gambo. On this point there is an interesting passage in Thomas Campion's preface to his first and second book of songs (q.v.), but we must not assume that Campion's methods were necessarily employed by other composers. From internal evidence it is clear that certain songs of Dowland and Jones were definitely conceived as four-part songs.

Robert Jones's first book of songs is dedicated ' To the honourable and virtuous gentleman Sir Robert (brother of Sir Philip) Sidney, Knight governour under Her Majesty of the town of Vlushing, and the castle of the Ramekins in the low countries, and of the forts of the same appendant, with the garrison therein placed as well of horse as foot ', in the following words :

' Your great love and favour, honourable Sir, ever manifested to all worthy sciences, hath emboldened me to offer up at your lordship's shrine these the unworthy labours of my musical travels. And though in respect of their weakness they may perhaps seem untimely brought forth, and therefore the unlikelier to prosper, yet doubt I not but if tendered by you they shall haply find gentle cherishing, which may be a mean to make them stronger, or else miscarrying, to encourage my endeavours to beget a better ; for as no art winks at fewer errors than music, so none greater enemies to their own profession than musicians, who whilst in their own singularity they condemn every man's works as some way faulty, they are the cause the art is the less esteemed and they themselves reputed as self-commenders and men most fantastical. Wherefore if this one censuring infirmity were removed, these my ayres (free I dare say from gross errors) would find everywhere more gracious entertainment. But since even those who are best seen in this art cannot vaunt themselves free from such detractors, I the less regard it, being so well accompanied. Howsoever if herein I may gain your honour's good allowance, I shall think I have attained to the better end of my labours, which with my self and the best of my service rests ever more at your lordship's employment.

Your lordship's devoted in all dutiful service,
ROBERT JONES.'

This is followed by an address *To the Reader :*

' Gentlemen, since my desire is your ears should be my indifferent judges, I cannot think it necessary to make my travels or my bringing up arguments to persuade you that I have a good opinion of myself, only thus much will I say, that I may prevent the rash judgments of such as know me not. Ever since I practised speaking I have practised singing ; having had no other quality to hinder me from the perfect knowledge of this faculty, I have been encouraged by the warrant of divers good judgments that my pains herein shall at the least procure good liking, if not delight, which yet for mine own part I must needs fear as much as I desire, especially when I consider the ripeness of this industrious age, wherein all men endeavour to know all things. I confess I was not unwilling to embrace the conceits of such gentlemen as were earnest to have me apparel these ditties for them : which though intended for their private recreation, never meaning they should come into the light, were yet content upon entreaty to make the encouragements of this my first adventure, whereupon I was almost glad to make my small skill known to the world, presuming that if my cunning failed me in the music, yet the words might speak for themselves, howsoever it pleaseth them to account better of that than of these, of purpose (as it should seem) to make me believe I can do something. My only hope is that seeing neither my cold ayres nor their idle ditties (as they will needs have me call them) have hitherto been sounded in the ears of many, they may chance to find such entertainment as commonly news doth in the world : which if I may be so happy to hear, I will not say my next shall be better, but I will promise to take more pains to shew more points of music, which now I could not do because my chiefest care was to fit the Note to the Word. Till when, I must be as well content with each man's lawful censure as I shall be glad of some men's undeserved favours.'

In common with all Jones's, and most of his contemporaries', song-books, this volume contains twenty-one songs. The precise significance of this figure is not clear, though the product of two such traditionally fortunate numbers as 3 and 7 may have been considered singularly propitious.

As a good example of the style of the work, the opening strain of No. 12, 'Farewell, dear love, since thou wilt needs be gone', may be quoted:

Example 16.

Fare - well,   dear   love, since thou wilt needs be   gone.

Mine   eyes do   show   my   life   is   al - most   done.

This is one of the snatches of song bawled out by Sir Toby Belch in *Twelfth Night* (II. iii), when Maria and Malvolio come in to protest against the shindy he and Sir Andrew are kicking-up in the middle of the night. The words are almost identical, and it seems likely that the tune Shakespeare knew was this one of Jones's, seeing that *Twelfth Night* was produced in the year following the production of Jones's book. The popularity of the song is attested by the appearance in the composer's fourth book, nine years later, of a song identical in metre and very similar in melody, 'Farewell, fond youth, if thou hadst not been blind'.

The Second Booke of Songs and Ayres, Set out to the Lute, the base Violl the playne way, or the Base by tableture after the leero fashion appeared in 1601. It is dedicated 'To the right virtuous and worthy Knight Sir Henry Leonard':

'Worthy Sir and my honourable friend, I give you this Child, I pray you bring it up, because I am a poor man and cannot maintain it. It may suffer much adversity in my name: your fortune may alter his stars and make him happy. Though his father be alive, I may call him an orphan, for poor men's children are Orphans born, and more to be pitied than they that have changed their fathers for their lands. Such may raise themselves in due time: we have no way to heighten our being but by another power. As gentlewomen peise themselves with tires and coronets, to appear more personable and tall, so must we add unto our littleness (if we will not be scorned for dwarfs) the crown of gentle persons more eminent and high. Our statures are not set above danger; we lie low, fit for every foot to tread upon, our place is the ground, there is nothing beneath us, and yet detraction will pull us lower if we have not good aspects. They will find means to dig and let us down into the earth and bury us before our time. This is the cause of patronage, and this is the persecution of them that would engross all glory into their own hands. But see the rage of these men, they bite the fruits themselves should feed upon. Virtue would bring forth many children but they hold them in the womb that they dare not come out. As the covetous man besiegeth all the land about him with statutes, fines and bands and other such like civil war, so doth the ambitious entrap the little portion of any commendations that may fall besides him; and like the merciless soldiers, the castles they cannot take, they blow up. They are as sparing of every small remnant of credit as if it were laid up in common-bank and the more were given away the less would come to their shares. They are miserable men: I will only brand them with this mark and let them go. They were eagles, if they did not catch flies; as they are, they are great things, much less than nothing. For my part, I will not contend with them; I desire no applause or commendations. Let them have the fame of echoes and sounds, and let me be a bird in your cage, to sing to myself and you. This is my content, and this my ambition. If I have this, I fail not in my expectation; if more for your sake, that is my advantage and I will owe you duty for it. In the meantime I rest

At your Worship's service,

ROBERT JONES.'

Two pages from Robert Jones's

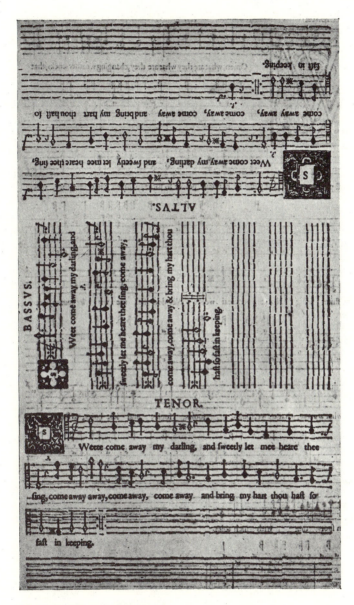

First Booke of Songs and Ayres, 1600.

The reader is addressed thus :

'Reader, I have once more adventured to ask thy counsel, whether I have done well or no in taking thus much pains to please thee. All that I will say for myself is : My intent towards thee was good, yet because perhaps I know thee not and I as yet am not grown so confident to warrant my endeavours against all men, I hold it no shame to crave uprightness in thy censure, as I mean not to accuse myself of negligence by begging thy favour : wherein I choose rather to deserve thy commendations than by my own praises to set my labours out to sale. The truth is, although I was not so idle when I composed these Ayres that I dare not stand to the hazard of their examination, yet I would be glad (if it might be) that thy friendly approbation might give me encouragement to sound my thankfulness more sweetly in thine ears hereafter. If the ditties dislike thee, 'tis my fault that was so bold to publish the private contentments of divers gentlemen without their consents, though (I hope) not against their wills : wherein if thou find anything to meet with thy desire, thank me, for they were never meant thee. I know not how the vulgar esteem travel [*sc.* travail = work], but methinks there should be no gentleman (when he may buy so much pains for so little money) that will not conclude he can at least be no loser by the bargain. If any musician will out of the pride of his cunning disdain me and these my beginnings as things not worth his envy, these are to desire him (if he be not grown past all charity) that he would accept the subscription of my name as a sufficient testimony that I am not ashamed of instruction, wherein soever I may appear to have outrun my justification. As for the rest that would fain inform men they know something by their general dislike of everything, I will not so much as desire them to be silent, lest I should hereby teach them at least how they might seem wise. For the book I will say only thus much : there hath not yet been any extant of this fashion which, if thou shalt pronounce to be but worth thy hearing, I rest satisfied, if not thy debtor. Farewell.'

If 'this fashion' designate a book of songs for one voice with instrumental accompaniment, the last statement is incorrect, for the preceding year had seen the publication of Morley's book of solo songs, and of the twenty-eight numbers in Cavendish's book (published in 1598) fourteen are for a single voice with the lute. Where Jones's second book is unique is in the provision of an alternative accompaniment for the bass viol tuned lyra- (leero) wise :

Example 17.

in addition to the usual lute tablature and bass viol part in ordinary notation for playing with the lute.

This book contains some of Jones's choicest and most original work. Particularly charming are the songs, ' Now what is love ',[1] with its fantastic harmonies (which are too clearly indicated in both tablatures to be misprints) and the delightful little four-note figure that haunts the last two lines of each verse :

Example 18.

It is per-haps that sanc-ing bell   That tolls us

---

[1] That this was the setting of Sir Walter Raleigh's lines which was sung in Thomas Heywood's *Rape of Lucrece* is shown by the appearance in the text of the play of the repetition of words that occurs in the last line of the song in Jones's version of the text, but not in the version printed in *England's Helicon* and elsewhere.

in - to Heav'n or Hell.

and '.Did ever man thus love as I ? ' with the delicious sequence in the fourth line :

Example 19.

I think I was made For no o - ther . .

trade, My mind

Other excellent songs in this book are ' Love's god is a boy ',
' Whither runneth my sweet heart ? ', and ' My love is neither
young nor old '.

The dedication of the madrigal set (to Robert Cecil, Earl of
Salisbury), published in 1607, is a not particularly brilliant example
of what Alfonso Ferrabosco the younger, a man ' not made of
much speech ', stigmatized as ' that solemn industry of many
in Epistles (to) enforce all that hath been said in praise of the
Faculty and make that commend the work '. But, in offering his
Ultimum Vale or the Third Booke of Ayres to Henry, Prince of
Wales, a year later, Jones's literary ability reasserted itself in this
admirable passage :

' Almost all our knowledge is drawn through the senses : they
are the soul's intelligencers whereby she passeth into the world
and the world into her, and amongst all of them, there is none
so learned as the ear, none hath obtained so excellent an art, so
delicate, so abstruse, so spiritual, that it catcheth up wild sounds
in the air and brings them under a government not to be expressed
but done, and done by no skill but its own. There is music in
all things, but every man cannot find it out, because of his own
jarring ; he must have a harmony in himself that should go about
it, and then he is in a good way, as he that hath a good ear is in
a good forwardness to our faculty. Conceit is but a well-tun'd
fancy, done in time and place : an excellent sentence is but
a well-tun'd reason well knit together : polity, or the subject
thereof, a commonwealth, is but a well-tun'd song where all
parts do agree and meet together, with full consent and harmony,
one serving other and every one themselves in the same labour.
But now I intrude into your art, in which all pray (and see hopes)
that God will give you a godly and prosperous knowledge, and
then all other arts shall prosper under it.'

But the popular little sportsman prince came to an untimely
end four years afterwards, and when his younger brother Charles
was on the throne, the ' commonwealth ' (fateful and prophetic
word !) was anything but a well-tuned song.

Ultimum Vale contains six admirable solo songs, followed by some duets and four-part ayres, including 'Thinkst thou, Kate, to put me down', which, though too frank a piece of bawdry for the modern concert-platform, has one of the best tunes Jones ever wrote—and all within the compass of a fifth :

Example 20.

Think'st thou, Kate, to put me down With a no or with a frown? Since love holds my heart in bands I must do, I must do, I must do as love com - mands.

The preface to this book seems to show that Jones had fallen upon evil times. 'I am set', he says, 'in an underfortune that hath need of friendship.'

Having taken his 'last farewell' of the musical public, the composer must have caused a certain amount of amusement when he came out with yet another book of songs within a twelve-month. One is reminded of certain 'farewell' concerts of modern times, and of Mr. Max Beerbohm, who followed up his *Works* with *More*, *Yet again*, and *And even now*. The excuse which Jones puts forward in the dedication (to Sir John Levinthorpe) of *A Musicall Dreame*, *Or the Fourth Booke of Ayres* is sufficiently humorous :

'It is not unknown unto your well-deserving self, Right Wor-shipful, that not long since I took my Ultimum Vale, with a resolving in myself never to publish any works of the same nature and fashion ; whereupon I betook me to the ease of my pillow, where Somnus having taken possession of my eyes and Morpheus the charge of my senses, it happened me to fall into a musical dream wherein I chanced to have many opinions and extravagant humours of divers natures and conditions, some of modest mirth, some of amorous love, and some of most divine contemplation. All these, I hope, shall not give any distaste to the ears or dislike to the mind, either in their words or in their several sounds, although it is not necessary to relate or divulge all dreams or phantasies that opinion begets in sleep or happeneth to the mind's apparition.'

But he had evidently come in for some hostile criticism since his last publication, for in place of the usual address to the reader we have here a page of savage invective against his detractors which even Mr. Josef Holbrooke could scarcely surpass :

To all Musical Murmurers this Greeting.

' Thou, whose ear itches with the variety of opinion, hearing thine own sound, as the echo, reverberating others' substance and unprofitable in itself, shews to the world comfortable noise, though to thy own use little pleasure by reason of uncharitable censure—I speak to thee, musical Momus, thou from whose nicety numbers as easily pass as drops fall in the shower, but with less profit. I compare thee to the highway dust that flies into men's eyes, and will not thence without much trouble, for thou in thy dispersed judgment not only art offensive to seeing knowledge but most faulty false to deserving industry, picking motes out of the most pure biss and smoothing the plainest velvet when only thine own opinion is more wrinkled and more vicious in itself than grosser soil, so that as a brush infected with filth thou rather soilest than makest perfect any way. I have stood at thine elbow and heard thee profane even music's best note and with thy untun'd relish Sol Fade most ignobly. I am assured, and I care not greatly, that thou wilt lay to my charge my whilom vow " never again " because I promised as much ; but understand me, thou unskilful descanter, derive from that note of plain song charitable numbers and thou shalt find harsh voices are often a note above E la reduced by truer judgment, which I bereave thee of, knowing thy rules are as our new-come lutes, being of many strings, not easily used, unless in adventure, till practise put forward into deserving division. This my adventure is no deed but a dream, and what are dreams but airy possessions and several ayres, breathing harmonious whisperings : though to thee discord, yet to others indifferent—I will not say excellent because it is another's office, not mine. But let them be as they are, others' profits and my pains, set forth for pleasure, not for purposed poison to infect imagination, no, but as a shower falling in a needful season, so I flatter myself at least and will say so ever by any other whose labour shall uplift musical meditation, the only wing of true courage being the most pleasing voice of man whose sweetness reacheth unto heaven itself. It is hard if all this pains reap not good commendations, and it is water wrung out of a flint in thee sith thou never thinkst well of any and wert in thyself so unskilful ever as thy tutor from the first hour could never make thee sing in tune. Be as thou art, a lump of deformity, without fashion, bred in the bowels of disdain, and brought forth by bewitch'd Megaera the fatal midwife to all true merit.

'Give me leave to depart, or if not, without it I am gone, careless of thy censuring and fully persuaded thou canst not think well and therefore art curst in thy cradle never to be but cruel, and being born with teeth in thy head bit'st every one harmless in this or what else honest industry makes thy ear gossip too.

'Farewell if thou wilt in kindness, or hold thyself from further carping.'

This book contains seven duets, eleven four-part ayres, and three solo songs, two of which have Italian words, the third being a breezy song about Robin Hood. In one of the duets occurs a reference to a very curious superstition that seems to have been current at the time, to the effect that 'she that dies a maid must lead an ape in Hell'. It is first mentioned in Lyly's *Euphues* (published in the middle of the reign of the Virgin Queen !) and crops up no fewer than four times in the song-books, viz. in Maynard's *XII. Wonders of the World*, Corkine's

Second Book of Ayres, Campion's song of ' the Fairy Queen Proser-
pina ' in the Rosseter book, and in the *Musical Dream.* There are
two references to it in Shakespeare (*Much Ado,* II. i. 43, and *Taming
of the Shrew,* II. i. 34), and it is to be met with also in *Drunken
Barnaby's Journal* and elsewhere. Its origin has yet to be explained.

Jones's last publication was another book of solo songs, *The
Muses' Gardin for Delights,* which appeared in 1610. The dedication to the Lady Wroth, daughter of Sir Robert Sidney by his
first wife, begins thus :

' Most honoured Lady, my eldest and first issue having thriv'd
so well under the protection of your right honourable father,
blame not this youngest and last babe if it desirously seek sanctuary
with yourself, as being a most worthy branch from so noble and
renowned a stock.'

and continues in the conventionally panegyrical manner. The
fit of spleen against the critics seems to have passed off, for this
time the preface is addressed *To the friendly Censurers ·*

' Dear friends, for so I call you if you please to accept my good
meaning, I presented you last with a Dream, in which I doubt
not but your fantasies have received some reasonable contentment : and now if you please to be awaked out of that Dream,
I shall for your recreation and refreshing guide you to the MUSES
GARDEN where you shall find such variety of delights that question-
less you will willingly spend some time in the view thereof. In
your first entrance into which Garden you shall meet with Love,
Love and nought but Love, set forth at large in his colours by
way of deciphering him in his nature. In the midst of it you
shall find Love rejected, upon inconstancy and hard measure of
ingratitude ; touching them that are lovers, I leave them to their
own censure in Love's description. And now for the end, it is
variable in another manner for the delight of the ear to satisfy
opinion. I am not so arrogant to commend mine own gifts,
neither yet so degenerate as to beg your toleration. If these
delights of flowers or variety of fruits may any way be pleasing
to your senses, I shall be glad. Otherwise I will vow never to
set, sow, plant or graft, and my labours henceforth shall cease

to trouble you. If you will needs mislike, I care not ; I will prevent your censures and defy your malice. If you despise me, I am resolute : if you use me with respect, I bid you most heartily

Farewell,

R. J.'

Twelve songs from this book, representing Jones at his best and blithest, are now available in print. Apart from their entrancing tunes, they are remarkable for the number of false relations and other harmonic piquancies they contain. The following quotation provides a good example as well as illustrating—in the cadence preceding the change of time-signature—a triple rhythm within the framework of the duple metre :

Example 21.

That once was high and got a . . fall.

O wil - low, wil - low, wil - low !

In 1614 Jones contributed three numbers to Sir William Leighton's *Tears or Lamentacions of a Sorrowfull Soule* (he had, in 1601, also contributed a madrigal to *The Triumphs of Oriana*). Otherwise, he gave no music to the world after 1610. In this year we find him associated with Philip Rosseter and two others as a director of the Children of the Queen's Revels,[1] the company of juvenile actors for whom Ben Jonson wrote *Cynthia's Revels* and *The Poetaster*. This was doubtless the company referred to with some acrimony in *Hamlet* (ii. ii) :

'. . . there is, Sir, an aiery of children, little eyases, that cry out on the top of question, and are most tyrannically clapped for 't : these are now the fashion, and so berattle the common stages—so they call them—that many wearing rapiers are afraid of goose-quills, and dare scarce come thither.'

Six years later a patent was granted to the four partners to erect a theatre on the site of the house, near Puddle Wharf, Blackfriars, where Jones was then residing. The house was pulled down and the theatre was well on the way to completion when the Lord Mayor and Aldermen of the City, growing alarmed at the increasing number of the theatres, raised an agitation against the project, which resulted in a royal edict ordering that the theatre be forthwith dismantled. After this we hear no more of Robert Jones, nor do we know when and where this genial person (in the English *and* German senses of the word) died and was buried.

[1] For a detailed account of this company see E. K. Chambers, *The Elizabethan Stage* (Clarendon Press), vol. ii, pp. 23–61.

5

Captain Tobias Hume

THE *homo unius libri* is a common enough figure in literary history, and in recent years anthologies have created, in many cases unjustly, a number of men of a single poem. Composers who are remembered for a single song are for the most part anonymous, though none the less definitely personal for that accident of fate. There are many folk-songs which are quite obviously the work of some particular singer of genius, and among the manuscripts and printed books of the sixteenth and seventeenth centuries we often find designated as 'D'Incerto' a song of such remarkable originality that it could not be attributed to any known composer of the period. Captain Tobias Hume, although he wrote much other music of only moderate interest, is fully entitled, on the strength of one perfect song, to a place in the annals of our music as secure as that which 'The Brooklet' has earned for Edward Loder, and 'To Anthea' for J. L. Hatton, among the song-writers of the nineteenth century.

Captain Hume, who appears to have been at one time a mercenary in the service of the King of Sweden, published two volumes of music. The first, which appeared in 1605 with the punning title of *Musicall Humors. The first part of Ayres, French, Pollish and others together, some in tabliture, and some in prickesong*, was dedicated to William, Earl of Pembroke, and contained a prefatory address in which the composer disclaims professionalism, and advocates the 'gambo violl' as a rival to the lute (which was then as generally used for the accompaniment of solo songs as the pianoforte is to-day) in the passage which was quoted with such bitter scorn seven years later by the unrivalled lutenist Dowland in his preface to *A Pilgrim's Solace*. Hume introduces himself thus *To the understanding Reader* :

' I do not study Eloquence, or profess Music, although I do love Sense and affect Harmony, my Profession being, as my Education hath been, Arms ; the only effeminate part of me hath been Music, which in me hath been always generous because never mercenary. To praise Music were to say the sun is bright. To extol my self would name my labours vain-glorious. Only this, my studies are far from servile imitations ; I rob no others' inventions, I take no Italian note to an English ditty, or filch fragments of songs to stuff out my volumes. These are mine own Fancies expressed by my proper *Genius*, which if thou dost dislike, let me see thine—*Carpere vel noli nostra, vel ede tua.* Now to use a modest shortness and a brief expression of my self to all noble spirits, thus : my title expresseth my book's contents, which (if my hopes fail me not) shall not deceive their expectation in whose approvement the crown of my labours resteth. And from henceforth the stateful instrument *Gambo Violl* shall with ease yield full various and as deviceful music as the lute. For here I protest the Trinity of Music, Parts, Passion and Division, to be as gracefully united in the Gambo Violl, as in the most received instrument that is : which here with a soldier's resolution I give up to the acceptance of all noble dispositions.

The friend of his friend,

Tobias Hume.'

It is a little difficult to reconcile the title of Hume's book with his claim that all the music it contains is of his own original composition.

Hume's songs are but seven in number, the greater part of his music being purely instrumental, but in their slender way they all show a certain originality of conception. There is a ' Soldier's Song ', with a very early example of battle onomatopoeia in the accompaniment, a very jovial ditty about tobacco which was still something of a novelty, a curious song described as ' The Imitation of Church Music, singing to the organs, but here you must use the Viol de Gambo for the organ ', and a hunting song which, as the composer proudly informs us, ' was sung before two Kings, to the admiring of all brave Huntsmen.'—

the occasion being the visit of the King of Denmark to the Court of James I in 1606. But it is his incomparable setting of that lovely anonymous poem, ' Fain would I change that note ' (which he alone has preserved for us), that has made him immortal, for this is one of the most perfect melodies ever penned by an Englishman. The poem has appeared frequently enough in anthologies, but one line in the second stanza has been given incorrectly both by A. H. Bullen and by Sir Arthur Quiller-Couch in the *Oxford Book of English Verse*, the word *ripe* being printed as *rich*.

Many of the instrumental pieces in this book have quaint descriptive titles, such as ' Tinckeldum Twinckeldum ', ' I am melancholy ', ' Tickle me quickly ', ' An English Frenchman ', ' Peter's Pleasure ', ' A snatch and away ', &c., and for the first time in English printed music expression marks and directions for interpretation are found. For example, at a certain point the words ' Play this pashenat ' (*sic*) appear, the succeeding passage being marked ' Play this as it stands ' ; and in another piece the player is instructed to ' Drum this with the back of the bow '— which is probably the first *col legno* in musical history.

His second book is entitled

' Captain Humes Poeticall Musicke. Principally made for two Basse-Viols, yet so contrived, that it may be plaied 8. severall waies upon sundrie Instruments with much facilitie. 1. The first way or musicke is for one Bass-Viole to play alone in parts, which standeth alwaies on the right side of this Booke. 2. The second musicke is for two Bass-Viols to play together. 3. The third musicke, for three Basse-Viols to play together. 4. The fourth musicke, for two Tenor Viols and a Basse-Viole. 5. The fift musicke, for two Lutes and a Basse-Viole. 6. The sixt musicke, for two Orpherions and a Basse-Viole. 7. The seventh musicke, to use the voyce to some of these musicks, but especially to the three Basse-Viols, or to the two Orpherions with one Basse-Viole to play the ground. 8. The eight and last musicke, is consorting all these Instruments together with the Virginals, or rather with a winde Instrument and the voice. 1607.'

The book opens with a collective dedication to the Queen (Anne of Denmark, wife of James I) :

' Thrice Royal Princess

' Since to commend music were but to reach the sun a pair of spectacles, or to extol my own endeavours would prove but superfluous gildings (since I hope they shall instantly come to the touch of your quick discovering judgment) I will only presume in most devoted zeal to offer up this last hope of my labours to your most princely acceptance, humbly imploring that it would please your thrice royal spirit not to esteem my songs unmusical because my fortune is out of tune, or to grant me little grace because my deserts may be valued nothing. But be once pleased, right excellent Princess, as the only and last refuge of my long expecting hopes to patronise and second the modest ends of the author of these uncommon musics, not for anything he yet can claim of just merit, but for what the ample gracings of the King and my excited affection to do your Majesty service may happily expect. I cease to offend your delicate ear with my harsh style, and therefore kissing the ground that sustaineth your sacred person, I ever rest

The humblest of your subjects

TOBIAS HUME.'

The ·British Museum copy of this book contains a pathetic postscript to this dedication in Hume's handwriting : ' I do in all humility beseech Your Majesty that you would be pleased to hear this music by me, having excellent instruments to perform it.'

Hume seems already to have fallen upon bad times, and it is plain that he left no stone unturned in his attempts to obtain patronage. Every instrumental piece in the *Poetical Music* bears a separate dedication to some person of rank, as is indicated by such sub-titles as ' The Lord Derry's favourite ', ' The Earl of Southampton's favourite ', ' The Duke of Lennox' delight ', &c. ; indeed his devotion to the nobility developed later into an intolerable importunity. In or about the year 1630 Hume presented a petition to the King asking permission to go, with 120 men, at the behest of the King of Sweden, to ' Mickle Bury Land ' (? Mecklenburg), and offering to deliver any letters King Charles may wish to send to the King of Sweden.

Already in his two music-books there are indications of an eccentric mind which in his last and only other publication is revealed as definitely unhinged. This is ' The true petition of Colonel Hume as it was presented to the Lords assembled in the High Court of Parliament ', and is an exceedingly fantastic document.

The humble petition of Tobias Hume, one of the poor brethren of that famous Foundation of the Charter House.

' *Right Honourable and Noble Lords,*

' I do humbly intreat to know why your Lordships do slight me, as if I were a fool or an Ass : I tell you truly I have been abused to your Lordships by some base fellows ; but if I did know them, I would make them repent it, were they never so great men in your sight ; for I can do the King's Majesty and my Country better service than the best Soldier or Colonel in this Land, or in all Christendom ; which now it is a great wonder unto me, that your Lordships do suffer so many unskilful Soldiers to go over for Ireland, to do the King's Majesties service, that are not able to lead a Company, neither do they know what belongs to a Soldier ; and yet for all this, your Lordships leave me out, that am able to do the King's Majesty better service than all the Soldiers that are now to be sent over for Ireland : so that if your Lordships please to pay for the making of a hundred or six score Instruments of war, which I am to have along with me, if you please to send me for Ireland, and make me Commander of all those men that are now to go over for Ireland, I will undertake to get in all Ireland in three or four Months at the farthest, or else if I do it not, I will give them leave to take off my head, if my Commanders will be as forward as my selfe, and yet I will do all things with great discretion. And I do here protest, I will do my King and my Country most true and faithful service, and give the first onset upon the Rebels in Ireland, to the honour

THE TRVE
PETITION
OF
COLONEL HVME,

As it was prefented to the Lords af-
fembled in the high Court of

PARLIAMENT:

Being then one of the poore Brethren of that famous Foundation
of the Charter. Houfe.

Declaring to their Lordfhips, that if they would
be pleafed to imploy him for the bufineffe in Ireland,
and let him have but fixfcore, or an hundred In-
ftruments of War, which he fhould give direction for to be made ; he would ruine
the Rebels all within three Months,
or elfe lofe his head.

Likewife he will undertake within three Months, if their
Lordfhips would but give credence to him, to bring
in by Sea, being furnifhed with a compleat Navy,
to his Majeftie and the Parliament 20.
Millions of Money.

London, Printed for *Iohn Giles*, 1 6 4 2.

1 4 Ialy

of all England : and therefore if you will not believe me, it is none of my fault, when I speak the truth : but if you will not give me the command of all the soldiers that go for Ireland at this time, I will not go for Ireland, but I will go for another Country, where I will have a greater command than all this which I have desired from your Lordships. But I yet live in hope that you will be pleased to believe me, and help me that live in great misery, by reason that I have maintained a thousand Soldiers in this City to do the King service in Ireland, and this I have done seven weeks together, which hath made me very poor, so that I have pawned all my best clothes, and have now no good garment to wear.

'And therefore I humbly beseech you all Noble Lords, that you will not suffer me to perish for want of food, for I have not one penny to help me at this time to buy me bread, so that I am like to be starved for want of meat and drink, and did walk into the fields very lately to gather Snails in the nettles, and brought a bag of them home to eat, and do now feed on them for want of other meat, to the great shame of this land, and those that do not help me, but rather command their servants to keep me out of their gates, and that is the Lord of Essex, and the Lord of Devonshire ; but I thank the good Lord of Pembroke, and the Lord Keeper, and the Earl of Hartford, and my Lord Mayor, and some other Knights, as Sir *John Worstenholm* and others do help me sometimes with a meal's meat, but not always, for I eat Snails and brown bread and drink small Beer, and sometimes water, and this I have thought good to make known unto your Lordships, hoping that your Honours will help me now with some relief, or else I shall be forced presently to run out of the land to serve another King, and do him all the great service, which I would rather do unto my own most gracious King, who would not suffer me to want, if I had money to bring me unto his Majesty, for I would do him true and faithful service in Ireland, and can do him very great service ; if his Majesty want money, I will undertake to fetch his Majesty home twenty millions of gold and silver in ready coin in the space of twelve or fourteen weeks : if this service be not worthy of meat and drink, judge you that are grave and wise Lords of the Parliament, for I will make no more Petitions unto your Lordships, for I have made many, but have not got any answer of them, and therefore if your

Lordships will neither entertain me, nor give me money to buy me meat and drink, I will go with as much speed as I can into other Countries, rather than I will be starved here. For I protest I cannot endure this misery any longer, for it is worse to me than when I did eat horse flesh, and bread made of the bark of trees, mingled with hay dust, and this was in Parno in List-land, when we were beleagured by the Polonians : but now to proceed further, I have offered to show your Lordships my instruments of war, and many other things which I can do fit for the wars, and yet other base fellows are set forward before me that cannot do the King's Majesty that great service which I can do him, and therefore I say it is a great shame to all this land, the Lord of Pembroke, the Lord *Craven*, and many other Lords and Knights and Gentlemen both in this Country and other Countries beyond the seas, as *Grave Maurice*, the Marquesse of Brunningburgh, and lastly the King of Swetheland, they all know that I am an old experienced Soldier, and have done great service in other foreign Countries, as when I was in Russia, I did put thirty thousand to flight, and killed six or seven thousand Polonians by the art of my instruments of war when I first invented them, and did that great service for the Emperor of Russia ; I do hereby tell you truly I am able to do my King and Country the best service of any man in Christendom, and I will maintain it with my art and skill, and with my sword in the face of all my enemies that do abuse me to the Lords of the Parliament and others, and if I did know them I would fight with them where they dare, and also disgrace them, I speak this, because I do hear that some of them have disgraced me unto some of the great Lords of the Parliament. Let those soldiers argue with me, and I will make fools of them all for matter of war, although they have persuaded the Lords to slight me, and therefore I say again, they are not able to do the King that good service which I can do him, both by sea and land.

' And so I humbly take my leave of your Lordships, being very desirous to speak with all the Lords of the Parliament, if they will vouchsafe to speak with me before I go out of this Land, for I am not able to endure this misery any longer, for I want money, meat and drink and clothes, and therefore I pray your Lordships to pardon my boldness, and help me with some relief if you please, or else I must of necessity go into other Countries presently, and so I most humbly take my leave for this time, and rest

Your Lordships most humble servant to do your Honours all the good service I can, for I have many excellent qualities I give God thanks for it.

TOBIAS HUME. Colonel.'

Three years later the poor mad captain (for he rose to no higher rank, save in his own imagination) died in the Charterhouse, where he had lived as a poor brother for fifteen years, a broken and a disappointed man.

6

Alfonso Ferrabosco the Younger

ALFONSO FERRABOSCO the Younger was born of Italian parents at Greenwich about the year 1575. His father, also named Alfonso, had come to England from his native town of Bologna some thirteen years previously, and had entered the service of Queen Elizabeth at whose Court he acquired a great reputation as a musician. The elder Ferrabosco was a prolific composer of madrigals, and a friend of William Byrd, with whom he had ' a virtuous contention in love made upon the plain-song of the *Miserere* ', and a competition on a secular theme which is mentioned by Henry Peacham in the *Compleat Gentleman* (1622) :

' Alfonso Ferrabosco the father, while he lived, for judgment and depth of skill (as also his son yet living) was inferior unto none ; what he did was most elaborate and profound, and pleasing enough in air, though Master Thomas Morley censoreth him otherwise. That of his " I saw my lady weeping " and " The Nightingale " (upon which ditty Master Byrd and he in a friendly emulation exercised their invention) cannot be bettered for sweetness of ayre or depth of judgment.'

Morley's censure of the older Ferrabosco has not survived, but this composer's ' deep skill ' is acknowledged in the *Plaine and easie Introduction to practicall Musicke* (1597). It is interesting to note that a song entitled ' I saw my lady weeping ' appears also in Morley's book of ayres, while Dowland's ' I saw my lady weep ' is one of the finest of all his songs.

In 1569 Ferrabosco *père* obtained temporary leave of absence from England. He went to Italy and, on one pretext after another, prolonged his visit for three years. In 1572 he was in England again, but six years later he returned to Italy and transferred his allegiance to the Duke of Savoy, regardless of the fact that he had bound himself never to leave the service of Queen Elizabeth. His children were left in the care of a certain Gomer van Awsterwyke, one of the Court musicians, and the Queen refused to let them leave England when their father sent for them some years after his departure. Perhaps she intended to hold them as hostages for the return of the truant ; but he never came back to England, and in 1588 he died in Turin.

The younger Alfonso, we learn from Anthony à Wood's manuscript notes on musicians which are preserved in the Bodleian Library :

' From his childhood was trained up to music, and at man's estate he became an excellent composer for instrumental music in the reign of King James I and King Charles I. He was most excellent at the Lira Viol and was one of the first that set lessons Lira-way to the Viol, in imitation of the old English Lute and Bandora. The most famous man in the world for fantazies of five and six parts.'

In 1604 we find him in the service of Prince Henry (the eldest son of King James I, who died young), for at Christmastide in that year he was granted a life pension of £50 a year ' in regard of his attendance upon the Prince and instructing him in the art of music '. He was also at that time one of the Extraordinary

Grooms of the Privy Chamber. During the next five years he frequently collaborated with Ben Jonson and Inigo Jones in the production of masques, the *Masque of Blackness* (1605), *Masque of Hymen* (composed for the marriage of Lord Essex and Lady Frances Howard (1607), the *Masque of Beauty* (1608), *Lord Haddington's Masque* (1608), and the *Masque of Queens* (1609), all containing songs by Ferrabosco. In the Description of the *Masque of Hymen* Ben Jonson expressed his admiration for the composer in a most enthusiastic passage (which was, however, omitted from the Folio edition of 1616) :

' And here, that no man's deservings complain of injustice (though I should have done it timelier I acknowledge), I do for honour's sake, and the pledge of our friendship, name Master Alfonso Ferrabosco, a man planted by himself in that divine sphere, and mastering all the spirits of music ; to whose judicial care and as absolute performance were committed all those difficulties both of song and otherwise, wherein what his merit made to the soul of our invention would ask to be expressed in tunes no less ravishing than his. Virtuous friend, take well this abrupt testimony, and think whose it is. It cannot be flattery in me who never did it to great ones ; and less than love and truth it is not, where it is done out of knowledge.'

In 1609 Ferrabosco published his two books : the *Ayres*, a book of twenty-eight songs and dialogues accompanied by lute and bass viol, and the *Lessons for 1. 2. and 3. viols*, both ' Printed by T. Snodham for John Brown, and are to be sold at his shop in Saint Dunstan's Churchyard in Fleet Street '. The *Ayres* are dedicated ' To the most equal to his birth, and above all titles but his own virtue: Heroic Prince Henry ', to whom in the previous year Robert Jones had dedicated his *Ultimum Vale* :

' Excellent Prince,
      ' That which was wont to accompany all sacrifices is now become a sacrifice : Music. And to a composition so full of harmony as yours, what could be a fitter offering ? The rather,

since they are the offerer's first-fruits, and that he gives them
with pure hands. I could now with that solemn industry of many
in Epistles enforce all that hath been said in praise of the Faculty,
and make that commend the work ; but I desire more the work
should commend the Faculty, and therefore suffer these few ayres
to owe their grace rather to your Highness' judgment than to
any other's testimony. I am not made of much speech ; only
I know them worthy of my name, and therein I took pains to
make them worthy of yours.

Your Highness' most humble servant

ALFONSO FERRABOSCO.'

This epistle dedicatory is followed by a poem of Ben Jonson
addressed ' To my excellent friend Alfonso Ferrabosco ' :

> To urge, my lov'd Alfonso, that bold fame
>   Of building towns and making wild beasts tame
> Which Music had, or speak her known effects,
>   That she removeth cares, sadness ejects, .
> Declineth anger, persuades clemency,
>   Doth sweeten mirth, and highten piety
> And is to a body often ill inclin'd
>   No less a sovereign cure than to the mind :
> To allege that greatest men were not asham'd
>   Of old even by her practice to be fam'd :
> To say, indeed, she were the soul of heaven
>   That the eight sphere, no less than planets seven
> Mov'd by her order, and the ninth, more high,
>   Including all, were thence called Harmony :
> I yet had utter'd nothing on thy part,
>   When these were but the praises of the art.
> But when I have said, The proofs of all these be
>   Shed in thy songs, 'tis true, but short of thee.

Thomas Campion also contributes some lines ' to the worthy
Author ' :

> Music's master and the offspring
>   Of rich music's father,
> Old Alfonso's image living,
>   These fair flowers you gather

Scatter through the British soil.
   Give thy fame free wing,
And gain the merit of thy toil.
   We whose loves affect to praise thee
   Beyond thy own deserts can never raise thee.

By T. Campion, Doctor in Physic.

Poetical tribute is also paid to the composer in a set of Latin Alcaics, signed N. (possibly Nathaniel, son of Thomas) Tomkins.

The *Lessons for Viols* are dedicated ' To the Perfection of Honour, my Lord Henry, Earl of Southampton ' (a notable patron of the arts, to whom Shakespeare and many another poet had paid homage), in the following words :

' Whilst other men study your titles (Honourable Lord) I do your honours, and find it a nearer way to give actions than words ; for the talking man commonly goes about, and meets the Justice at his error's end, not to be believed. Yet, if in modest actions the circumstances of singularity and profession hurt not, it is true that I made these compositions solely for your Lordship, and do here profess it : by which time I have done all that I had in purpose, and return to my silence,

Where you are most honoured
by

ALFONSO FERRABOSCO.'

Then follow (1) an address *To the World* :

' Lest I fall under the character of the vainglorious man, in some opinions, by thrusting so much of my industry in print, I would all knew how little fame I hope for that way, when beside his, for, and to whom they are, I aimed at no man's suffrage in the making, though I might presume that could not but please others which I was contented had pleased him. But as it is the error and misfortune of young children oftentimes to stray, and losing their dwellings, be taken up by strangers and there loved and owned, so these, by running abroad, having got them false parents —and some that to my face would challenge them—I had been a most unnatural father if I had not corrected such impudence, and by a public declaration of them to be mine (when other means abandoned me) acknowledged kind. This is all the glory I affected, to do an act of nature and justice. For their seal, they had it in the mint or not at all; howsoever, if they want it, I will ease myself the vice of commendation.'

(2) A sonnet by Ben Jonson, again addressed ' To my excellent friend ' :

> When we do give, Alfonso, to the light
> A work of ours, we part with our own right,
> For then all mouths will judge, and their own way,
> The Learn'd have no more privelege than the Lay.
> And though we could all men, all censures hear
> We ought not give them taste we had an ear ;
> For if the humorous world will talk at large,
> They should be fools, for me, at their own charge.
> Say this or that man they to thee prefer,
> Even those for whom they do this know they err,
> And would (being ask'd the truth) ashamed say
> They were not to be nam'd on the same day.
> Then stand unto thyself, nor seek without
> For Fame, with breath soon kindled, soon blown out.

and (3) an Italian sonnet, signed *Gual: Quin.*

Little remains to be recorded of Ferrabosco's life. On the death of Prince Henry in 1612 his services were transferred to the new Prince of Wales (who afterwards became King Charles I). In 1614 he contributed three anthems to Sir William Leighton's *Teares or Lamentacions of a Sorrowfull Soule.* In 1619 a grant was made

' for 21 years to Alfonso Ferrabosco, Innocent Lanier and Hugh Lydiard for cleansing the River of Thames of flats and shelves which annoy the same to the prejudice of navigation, with a grant of such fines and forfeitures as shall be forfeited to His Majesty upon the statutes of 27 and 34 of King Henry the Eight by any persons for annoying the said river, with power to them to sell the sand and gravel they shall take out of the Thames to brickmakers or others at usual prices. There is an allowance to them of one penny per ton of stranger's goods and merchandises to be imported and exported into or out of the Port of London in ships or other vessels. Done by order from Mr. Secretary Calvert, Subscr. by Mr. Attorney General.'

Ferrabosco afterwards sold his share in the Patent ' for a great sum of money '.

In 1623 he was appointed one of the King's Musicians, a position he retained when, two years later, Charles I succeeded to the throne ; in 1626, on the death of John Cooper (Coprario), he became Composer of Music in Ordinary ; and in 1628 he died at Greenwich, and was buried on the 11th of March in the parish church where Thomas Tallis had been laid to rest forty-three years before.

There is no evidence that the younger Ferrabosco ever left England, and it is not at all unlikely that he lived all his life at Greenwich, where he is known to have spent his last years ; so we may with justice claim him as an English composer. Like his friend Ben Jonson, he was, as we see from his prefaces, something of a plain, blunt Englishman. There are, however, distinct traces of Italian influences in his compositions. It is significant that of all the composers of ayres in this period, only Ferrabosco and John Cooper, who spent many years of his life in Italy, are entirely non-modal in their harmonic outlook, and both of these composers rely exclusively on the voice for their expressive effects. When Ferrabosco becomes declamatory, after the manner of the so-called ' new music ' in Italy, he is merely dull and uninspired. At his best he is a melodist and not a monodist. His vocal line is generally smooth, graceful, and shapely, and although his music never rises to any great intensity, he now and again achieves an emotional utterance of real beauty by very simple means, as in the lovely cadence of the song, ' Like hermit poor ' :

Example 22.

To let in Death when Love and For - tune, when

Love and For - - - - - tune will.

There is a good deal of chamber music for viols by Ferrabosco to be found in the manuscript collections at Oxford. This has been described by Dr. Ernest Walker in an interesting article in the *Musical Antiquary* for January 1912, and Mr. G. E. P. Arkwright has written a very detailed account of the whole Ferrabosco family in an essay contributed to Robin Grey's *Studies in Music*, to which I am indebted for much of the information given in these pages.

7

Thomas Campion[1]

MR. PERCIVAL VIVIAN has written so admirable and definitive
an account of Campion's life and works in his collected edition
of the poet's writings, published by the Clarendon Press (and,
in shorter form, in his edition of Campion for Routledge's 'Muses
Library '), that a brief summary of the few facts definitely known
about his life is all that is needed here. He was born on the
12th of February 1567, and was christened in St. Andrew's Church,
Holborn. His grandfather was a Dublin man, so the poet may
have had Irish blood in him. His father died when he was nine
years old, and his mother married again, but did not long survive.
Campion's education was undertaken by his step-father, Augustine
Steward, who sent him to Cambridge in 1582 ; but he left without
taking any degree—a fact which suggests that he may have been
a Roman Catholic. He was admitted to Gray's Inn in 1586,
and at some later date he took up the study of medicine and
obtained the degree of M.D., presumably at some foreign university. Although he published no English verse until 1601, his
poetry had been widely circulated in manuscript copies, and by
1593 he had already achieved some reputation as a poet, for
George Peele refers to him as one 'that richly clothes conceit
with well-made words ' in his *Honour of the Garter* which was
published in that year. In 1595 he published a book of Latin
Epigrams, which contains a poem in praise of John Dowland,
and two years later he wrote another laudatory epigram for
publication in Dowland's *First Book of Ayres*. In 1601 appeared
Philip Rosseter's *Book of Ayres*, to which Campion contributed
both words and music of twenty-one of the forty-two songs the
book contains, and almost indubitably supplied the words of the

---

[1] The spelling *Campion* has been adopted, as being that most frequently
used by the poet himself, although *Campian* is found in two of his musical
publications.

remaining twenty-one songs which were set to music by Philip
Rosseter. It is probable that the following address *To the reader*
is also from the pen of Campion :

' What epigrams are in poetry, the same are ayres in music,
then in their chief perfection when they are short and well
seasoned. But to clog a light song with a long praeludium is to
corrupt the nature of it. Many rests in music were invented,
either for necessity of the fugue, or granted as an harmonical
licence in songs of many parts ; but in airs I find no use they
have, unless it be to make a vulgar and trivial modulation seem
to the ignorant, strange : and to the judicial, tedious. A naked
ayre without guide or prop or colour but his own is easily censured
of every ear, and requires so much the more invention to make
it please. And as Martial speaks in defence of his short epigrams,
so may I say in the apology of ayres : that where there is a full
volume, there can be no imputation of shortness. The lyric poets
among the Greeks and Latins were first inventors of ayres, tying
themselves strictly to the number and value of their syllables, of
which sort you shall find here only one song in Sapphic verse ;
the rest are after the fashion of the time, ear-pleasing rhymes,
without art. The subject of them is, for the most part, amorous :
and why not amorous songs, as well as amorous attires ? Or why
not new ayres, as well as new fashions ?

' For the note and tablature, if they satisfy the most, we have
our desire ; let expert masters please themselves with better.
And if any light error hath escaped us, the skilful may easily
correct it, the unskilful will hardly perceive it. But there are
some who, to appear the more deep and singular in their judgment, will admit no music but that which is long, intricate,
bated with fugue, chained with syncopation, and where the
nature of every word is precisely expressed in the note : like the
old-exploited action in comedies, when if they did pronounce
Memini, they would point to the hinder part of their heads ; if
Video, put their finger in their eye. But such childish observing
of words is altogether ridiculous, and we ought to maintain as
well in notes as in action, a manly carriage, gracing no word,
but that which is eminent and emphatical. Nevertheless, as in
poesy we give the pre-eminence to the Heroical Poem, so in

music we yield the chief place to the grave and well invented Motet, but not to every harsh and dull confused Fantasy, where in multitude of points the harmony is quite drowned.

' Ayres have both their art and pleasure, and I will conclude of them as the poet did in his censure of Catullus the Lyric, and Virgil the Heroic writer :

> ' Tantum magna suo debet Verona Catullo,
>   quantum parva suo Mantua Virgilio.'

The dedication, to Sir Thomas Monson, which is signed by Rosseter, explains that these songs of Campion, like those of Dowland's first book, had been composed several years before publication :

' Sir, The general voice of your worthiness, and the many particular favours which I have heard Master Campion with dutiful respect, often acknowledge himself to have received from you, have emboldened me to present this Book of Airs to your favourable judgment and gracious protection ; especially because the first rank of Songs are of his own composition, made at his vacant hours, and privately imparted to his friends, whereby they grew both public, and as coin cracked in exchange, corrupted, some of them, both words and notes, unrespectively challenged by others. In regard of which wrongs, though his self neglects these light fruits as superfluous blossoms of his deeper studies, yet hath it pleased him, upon my entreaty, to grant me the impression of part of them, to which I have added an equal number of mine own. And this two-faced Janus, thus in one body united, I humbly entreat you to entertain and defend, chiefly in respect of the affection which I suppose you bear him who, I am assured, doth above all others love and honour you. And for my part I shall think myself happy if in any service I may deserve this favour.

' Your Worship's humbly devoted,

'Philip Rosseter.'

In 1602 Campion published his *Observations in the Art of English Poesy*, in which he inveighs—curiously enough—against ' the vulgar and unartificial custom of riming ' in English poetry and advocates the cultivation of quantitative verse without rhyme, in metres derived from those of the Latin and Greek classics. He was answered in the same year by Samuel Danyel in *An Apologie for Ryme* (these two little works have recently been reprinted together as one volume of *The Bodley Head Quartos*), and Ben Jonson is said to have written a *Discourse of Poesy* directed ' both against Campion and Danyel ', but this work has not survived. In 1605 Campion is mentioned by William Camden in a list of the best English poets of the time which includes Sidney, Spenser, and Shakespeare, and in the following year appears the first reference to Campion as a ' Doctor in physic '. In 1607 he wrote a Masque in honour of the marriage of Lord Hayes, to which he also contributed the music of two songs, the rest of the music being composed by Thomas Lupo and Thomas Childs, the organist of St. Paul's Cathedral. Apart from the poem prefixed to Ferrabosco's *Book of Ayres*, which has been already quoted, his next publication was a book of *Songs of Mourning : Bewailing the untimely death of Prince Henry*. These lyrics were not set to music by Campion himself, but by John Cooper, or, as he chose to call himself, Coprario. In the same year (1613) Campion wrote three more Masques, to which, however, he contributed no music, and it is possible that 1613 is the date to be assigned to

' Two Books of Airs.   The First containing Divine and Moral Songs : The Second, Light Conceits of Lovers.   To be sung to the Lute and Viols, in two, three, and four Parts : or by one Voice to an Instrument.'

There is no date on the title-page, but as the last song in the first book is an elegy on the death of Prince Henry (or ' Hally ' as he is here called), which took place on the 6th of November 1612, one may assume that the book was issued soon after this event.

The address *To the reader* is a most illuminating little essay on the composition of ayres and on the proper relation between music and poetry :

'Out of many songs which, partly at the request of friends, partly for my own recreation, were by me long since composed, I have now enfranchised a few, sending them forth divided, according to their different subjects, into several books. The first are grave and pious : the second, amorous and light. For he that in publishing any work hath a desire to content all palates must cater for them accordingly.

Non omnibus unum est
quod placet ; hic spinas colligit, ille rosas.

These ayres were for the most part framed at first for one voice with the lute or viol : but upon occasion they have since been filled with more parts, which whoso please may use, who like not may leave. Yet do we daily observe that when any shall sing a treble to an instrument, the standers-by will be offering at an inward part out of their own nature ; and, true or false, out it must, though to the perverting of the whole harmony. Also, if we consider well, the treble tunes (which are with us commonly called ayres) are but tenors mounted eight notes higher ; and therefore an inward part must needs well become them, such as may take up the whole distance of the diapason, and fill up the gaping between the two extreme parts : whereby though they are not three parts in perfection, yet they yield a sweetness and content both to the ear and mind, which is the aim and perfection of Music.

' Short ayres, if they be skilfully framed and naturally expressed, are like quick and good epigrams in poesy, many of them showing as much artifice, and breeding as great difficulty as a larger poem. Non omnia possumus omnes, said the Roman epic poet. But some there are who admit only French or Italian ayres ; as if every country had not his proper ayre, which the people thereof naturally usurp in their music. Others taste nothing that comes forth in print ; as if Catullus' or Martial's Epigrams were the worse for being published.

' In these English ayres, I have chiefly aimed to couple my words and notes lovingly together, which will be much for him to do

that hath not power over both. The light of this will best appear
to him who hath paysed our monosyllables and syllables combined, both of which are so loaded with consonants, as that
they will hardly keep company with swift notes, or give the vowel
convenient liberty.

‘ To conclude : my own opinion of these songs I deliver thus:
   Omnia nec nostris bona sunt, sed nec mala libris ;
   si placet hac cantes, hac quoque lege legas.
                                        Farewell.’

In 1616 we find Campion attending, in his professional capacity
as a doctor of medicine, upon Sir Thomas Monson, who had been
imprisoned in the Tower for his alleged complicity in the murder
of Sir Thomas Overbury. Monson was released two years later,
and this enables us to date the otherwise undated

‘ Third and Fourth Book of Ayres : composed by Thomas Campian. So as they may be expressed by one Voice, with a Viol,
Lute, or Orpharian.’

for the third book contains a dedication in verse to Sir Thomas
Monson, which begins with the words :

   Since now those clouds, that lately overcast
   Your fame and fortune, are dispers’d at last.

The fourth book is dedicated to Monson’s son, and in the address
To the Reader Campion, rather surprisingly, forestalls criticism
of the moral tone of some of his verses :

‘ The apothecaries have books of gold, whose leaves, being
opened, are so light as that they are subject to be shaken with
the least breath ; yet rightly handled, they serve both for ornament and use. Such are light ayres.

‘ But if any squeamish stomachs shall check at two or three
vain ditties in the end of this book, let them pour off the clearest
and leave those as dregs in the bottom. Howsoever, if they be
but conferred with the Canterbury Tales of that venerable poet
Chaucer, they will then appear toothsome enough.

‘ Some words are in these books, which have been clothed in
music by others, and I am content they then served their turn :
yet give me now leave to make use of mine own. Likewise you

may find here some three or four songs that have been published before ; but for them, I refer you to the Players' bill, that is styled : *Newly revived, with Additions*, for you shall find all of them reformed, either in words or notes.

' To be brief. All these songs are mine, if you express them well ; otherwise they are your own. Farewell.

'Yours, as you are his,

'THOMAS CAMPIAN.'

Campion's last publication was an admirable little treatise on counterpoint which was many times reprinted later in the century by Playford, and might well be used to-day by students of composition in preference to many a modern text-book. Nothing could show more clearly the change that was coming over musical thought in the first quarter of the seventeenth century than a comparison of this clear and lucid little book with the treatise of Ornithoparcus which Dowland translated, or even Morley's *Plain and easie Introduction to practicall Musicke*. It is therefore a little surprising to find a poem of Campion prefixed to Thomas Ravenscroft's *Brief Discourse of the true (but neglected) use of Charact'ring the Degrees by their Perfection, Imperfection and Diminution in Mensurable Music* (1614), the last belated plea for the retention of the medieval conception of musical theory. It may be, however, that Campion only supplied this poem to oblige an old friend, for he expresses a somewhat qualified approval of Ravenscroft's work in these lines :

> The Marks that limit music here are taught,
> So fixed of old, which none by right can change,
> Though Use much alteration hath wrought,
> To Music's fathers that would now seem strange.

Campion died on the 1st of March 1620 and was buried at St. Dunstan's-in-the-West, Fleet Street. He did not make a formal will, but almost with his last breath he said ' that he did give all that he had unto Mr. Philip Rosseter and wished that his estate had been far more or uttered words to that effect '.

Mr. Philip Rosseter benefited by the worthy doctor to the extent of £22.

Campion is the most prolific of all the song-writers, having no fewer than 118 ayres to his credit, but although it is probable that all his English lyrics were written expressly for music, it cannot be said that Campion is as distinguished a composer as he is a poet. His poetical works can be read through with enjoyment from the first page to the last, but when one reads through the music with which they are allied, one experiences a certain feeling of disappointment. This, of course, is largely due to the superlative excellence of the poems. Campion is primarily an inventor of deliciously pretty tunes, and his ingenuity as a metrist is often reflected in very pleasant devices of rhythm in their construction. Good examples may be seen in ' Her rosy cheeks ' in the second book and ' O never to be moved ' in the third. On the other hand, there are too many complacently four-square songs of the conventional hymn-tune pattern to be found in Campion's song-books, and many of these are of so slight a substance that they come dangerously near to sheer triviality. Extreme neatness of workmanship is always apparent in the music as in the poems ; but there is a complete absence of any deeper quality than surface charm in the music, where the words demand a certain measure of intensity for their adequate expression.

But this is rather carping criticism. There is so much to delight and charm us in this fragile music that it is ungracious to cavil at it for the lack of qualities which we can find in abundance elsewhere. There are many attractively gay little ditties in these books, of which ' Jack and Joan ' (Book I), ' A secret love or two ' (Book III), ' I care not for these ladies '—an enchanting little tune in the manner of a country dance—in the Rosseter book, ' There is a garden in her face ' (Book IV), and ' Fain would I wed ' (Book IV), may be mentioned as typical examples. The last-named song is cast in the unusual form of a short set of vocal variations on a recurring harmonic ground. A transcription of the tune, by Richard Farnaby, appears in the Fitzwilliam Virginal Book. Perhaps Campion is seen at his best in half-serious songs such as ' When to her lute Corinna sings ', ' Shall I come, sweet love, to thee ? ', and ' Love me or not ', in which a certain tender grace is mingled with a rather wistful vein of sentiment.

8

Philip Rosseter

PHILIP ROSSETER is revealed in his songs as one of the most attractive personalities of the whole period of the English Ayre, but we know singularly little about him. We have no information about his life prior to 1601, when he and Campion published their joint *Book of Airs*. This book was offered for sale at Rosseter's house ' in Fleet Street near to the Gray-hound '. His only other publication was a book of

' Lessons for Consort, made by sundry excellent authors and set to sixe severall instruments. Namely, the Treble Lute, Treble Violl, Base Violl, Bandora, Citterne and the Flute. 1609.'

This work was inspired by the success of Thomas Morley's *Consort Lessons* for the same combination of instruments, which had appeared ten years earlier—the first example of instrumental chamber-music to be published in England. Both of these works were issued in separate part-books, and unfortunately no complete set of either of them has survived—though it is always possible that the missing parts may come to light at some future time. The cittern and bandora were plucked instruments with strings of wire, playing treble and bass parts respectively in the Consort. Morley's book was dedicated to the Lord Mayor and Aldermen of the City of London, and his preface gives a good account of the purposes for which it was made :

'The songs are not many, lest too great plenty should breed
a scarceness of liking : they be not all of one kind, because men's
fantasies seek after variety : they be not curious, for that men
may by diligence make use of them : and the exquisite musician
may add in the handling of them to his greater commendation.
They be set for divers instruments, to the end that whose skill
or liking regardeth not the one, may attempt some other. The
pain is passed in the hope to procure your Lordships' pleasure
and recreation. . . . As the ancient custom of this most honourable and renowned city hath been ever to retain and maintain
excellent and expert musicians to adorn your honours' favours,
feasts and solemn meetings, to those your Lordships' WAYTS,
after the commending these my labours to your honourable
patronage, I recommend the same to your servants' careful and
skilful handling, that the wants of exquisite harmony, apparent,
being left unsupplied, for brevity of proportions, may be excused
by their melodious additions.'

The book contains arrangements of several of Dowland's songs :
Captain Piper's Pavan ('If my complaints'), 'Can she excuse
my wrongs', which is described as a Galliard, 'Now O now
I needs must part' (here called 'the Frog Galliard'), and the
'Lachrimae' Pavan.

Rosseter describes the pieces in his book as 'flowers gathered
out of divers gardens, and now by me consorted and divulged
for the benefit of many'. By 'consorted' he means arranged
for this particular combination of instruments which was, we
learn, available in the household of Sir William Gascoyne of
Sedbury, to whom the book is dedicated. In the address *To the
Reader* Rosseter acknowledges his indebtedness to Morley and
the other composers represented in the book :

'The good success and frank entertainment which the late
imprinted set of Consort books generally received hath given me
encouragement to second them with these my gatherings, most
of the songs being of their inventions whose memory only remains,
because I would be loth to rob any living men of the fruit of their
own labours, not knowing what private intent they may have to

convert them to their more peculiar use. The authors' names I have severally prefixed, then every man might obtain his right; and as for my industry in disposing them, I submit it to thy free censure.'

The book contains twenty-five pieces : two by Rosseter himself —a Pavan and Galliard; three by Morley, among them 'Now is the month of May'; a piece by Campion entitled 'Move on'; and compositions by Anthony Holborne, John Baxter, Thomas Lupo, Richard Allison, and John Farmer.

In 1604 Rosseter was one of the King's musicians for the lute, and on the title-page of the *Consort Lessons* of 1609 he is still described as such. After the publication of this book he entered the theatrical world. On the 4th of January 1610 a patent was granted to him, with Robert Jones and two others, ' to provide, keep and bring up a convenient number of children, and them to practise and exercise in the quality of playing, by the name of Children of the Revels to the Queen, within the Whytefryars in the suburb of our city of London, or in any other convenient place '.

In 1612 and 1613 Rosseter's company, in conjunction with the Lady Elizabeth's company, performed a number of plays under Rosseter's direction, amongst them Ben Jonson's *Epicoene*, Nathaniel Field's *A Woman is a Weathercock*, and George Chapman's *Widow's tears*. For each performance Rosseter was allowed about £6. On the 31st of May 1615 Rosseter and his three partners obtained a licence to build a new theatre at their own expense for the use of the Children, the Prince's Players, and the Lady Elizabeth's Players. The building was begun in the autumn of that year and by January 1616 was ' almost, if not fully, finished '. But the Corporation of London objected to the opening of yet another theatre in the City and, invoking King James's authority, compelled the licensees to render their building unfit for the use for which it was designed. Rosseter is said to have associated himself with the Lady Elizabeth's Players after this occurrence, but he is not known to have taken any important part in their productions, and we hear no more of him until his death on the 5th of May 1623. He was buried at St. Dunstan's-in-the-West, near his old friend Thomas Campion.

On the 5th of May 1923 the three hundredth anniversary of his death was commemorated by a song recital at Steinway Hall, London, by the late Philip Wilson.

It is difficult to account for the curious fascination of Rosseter's music. It is almost all ' still-music '. His songs are so slight, yet so insinuating ; their charm grows on one. They have the fragrance of old-world gardens, the mellow beauty of certain portraits of women of a bygone age with quiet wisdom in their eyes ; they are a little remote, they trouble the mind like half-remembered things. Campion himself could not embody his verses so perfectly in music as did his friend.

> Though far from joy, my sorrows are as far,
> And I both between

expresses the prevailing mood of the book. ' When Laura smiles ' is set to a merry tune, and there is mockery in ' If she forsake me ' and ' Whether men do laugh or weep '.

It is possible to express as much in ten bars as in a symphony. There may be greater songs than this, but none more near perfection in its kind.

Example 23.

What then is love but mourn - ing?

What de - sire but a self - burn - ing?

Till she that hates doth love re - turn,

Thus will I mourn, thus will I sing,

Come a - way, come a - way, my dar - ling.

9

Cavendish, Greaves, Corkine, Ford, Pilkington, and Morley

ONE of the most interesting music-books of the whole of this period is the book of

' 14 Ayres in Tabletorie to the Lute expressed with two voyces and the base Violl or the voice and Lute only. 6 more to 4 voyces and in Tabletorie. And 8 Madrigalles to 5 voyces. . . 1598.'

This work had long been known to exist, and in the eighteenth century one number was reprinted from it in one of Longman and Broderip's collections of madrigals and glees, but recent bibliographers had given it up for lost until a copy unexpectedly turned up at the Britwell Court sale in 1918 and was purchased for the British Museum. It is not a perfect exemplar, the title-page and two pages of music being damaged, but we are very fortunate in possessing a copy at all, for had this book perished, we should have lost one of the treasures of English music.

Cavendish describes himself simply as a ' Gentleman ' in this book, so we may conclude that he was not a professional musician. He was a member of the Cavendish family, the head of which became Duke of Devonshire in later times. His grandfather was George Cavendish, of Cavendish Manor in Suffolk, from which place he inscribes the dedication of his book to his second cousin, Lady Arabella Stuart (daughter of Charles Stuart, Earl of Lennox, and younger brother of Lord Darnley), who was the next heir to the English throne after her first cousin, James VI of Scotland.

' Many causes I have to embolden mine attempts of duty to you, and your favours stand in the top of them ; others there are more secret, and lie in the nature of your own apprehension. And howsoever the policy of times may hold it unfit to raise men humbled with adversities to titles of dearness, whether to shun charge or express pride I rather know not, yet you, I hope, out of the honour of your nature will vouchsafe your favours to a forward servant so nearly tied to a dutiful devotion.'

The book is unique in that it contains under one cover accompanied solo ayres, four-part ayres to be sung with the lute (but whether the lute was to be used when all four voices were present or merely when these ayres were sung as solos is not clear), and eight five-part madrigals without accompaniment. There is no very marked difference in style between the ayres and the madrigals ; indeed, two numbers, ' Wandering in this place ' and ' Every bush new springing ', are given in both forms, first as accompanied solo ayres and afterwards as madrigals. It is, however, fairly clear that they were originally conceived as madrigals. Another of the madrigals, ' Come, gentle swains ', was reprinted, after considerable revision, in *The Triumphs of Oriana*, three years after its initial publication.

The general level of the music in this book is consistently high ; there are no really dull or feeble numbers, such as we find in plenty in the works of Jones, Ferrabosco, Bartlet, Hume, and others. Although these are actually the earliest songs for solo voice and lute published in England, Cavendish's technique is quite mature enough to enable him to strike a very personal note in his work. One or two of the serious songs, such as ' The heart to rue the pleasure of the eye ' and ' Fair are those eyes ', are amongst the best things of their kind in this period ; the lighter four-part ayres are delicious trifles, of thoroughly sound workmanship, ' Every bush new springing' is quite worthy to rank with the best of Morley's ballets, and the solo song ' Down in a valley ' is a charming and wholly original production.

Apart from a few numbers contributed to Este's *Whole Book of Psalmes* in 1592, no other compositions of Cavendish are known, unless he is to be identified with ' Mr. Candish ', some of whose lute music appears in manuscript collections.

Thomas Greaves

The only published work of Thomas Greaves is, like that of Cavendish, of a composite nature. It is described as

' Songs of sundrie kindes : First, Aires to be sung to the Lute, and Base Violl. Next, Songes of sadnesse, for the Viols and Voyce. Lastly, Madrigalles for five voyces. 1604.'

Greaves was a lutenist in the service of Sir Henry Pierrepoint, of Holm in Nottinghamshire, to whom his book is dedicated. No further details of his life are known ; but it appears, from some commendatory verses prefixed to his work, that, unlike most other musicians of his time, he spent most of his life in the country, that he was already growing old when his book was published, and that the works contained in it had existed in manuscript for many years before they were printed. ' Celestina ', ' Flora ', and ' I pray thee, sweet John, away ' are very pleasant songs of a light pastoral character, and the songs with viols are quite attractive in a gentle unassuming sort of way. The first of them is written for a voice of the remarkable compass of an octave and seven notes. They are the earliest English songs with string-quartet accompaniment to be printed with a specific designation that they were intended as such, and were not merely compositions ' apt for voices or viols '. But the appearance of one song (' Buy new broom ') in Thomas Whythorne's *Songes of three, fower, and five voyces* (1571), with words only in the treble part, makes it clear that it was intended to be sung as a solo with string-quartet accompaniment ; and William Byrd writes in the preface to his *Psalmes, Sonets, and Songs of Sadness and pietie* (1588) : ' Here are divers songs which being originally made for instruments to express the harmony and one voice to pronounce the ditty, are now framed in all parts for voices to sing the same.'

William Corkine

The two published works of William Corkine contain both songs and instrumental pieces for the lyra viol, a smaller instrument than the bass viol, tuned to a chord and written for in tablature like the lute. The first book, in which the songs are for solo voice to the accompaniment of lute and bass viol, was published in 1610. In the course of his dedication ' To the two honourable knights, Sir Edward Herbert, of the noble order of the Bath, and Sir William Hardy ', Corkine says :

' It was long before the use of notes and tablature came into our English press, but having found the way, there are few nations yield more impressions in that kind than ours, every musician according to his ability increasing the number.'

The second book, published in 1612, is divided into sections, each with a separate dedication, for which Corkine thus apologizes :

' As a poor man, indebted to many and desirous to pay what he can, divides that little he hath among many, to give contentment at least to some, so I am constrained to make the like distribution of this poor mite of mine, being all that I have, for the present, to content you my worthiest creditors.'

Corkine's talent as a song-writer is a slender one, but some of his songs are agreeable enough, particularly ' Sweet let me go ', ' Shall a frown or angry eye ', and ' Some can flatter ' in the first book. It is interesting to note that whereas the songs in the first book are directed to be sung ' to the Lute *and* Bass Viol ', some of those in the second book are accompanied by the bass viol alone in single notes, though in this book, too, there are songs to be sung to the lute *and* bass viol. As this book also contains instrumental music for the lyra viol—an instrument which permitted some kind of harmonic filling-up of the melody it played—(and this filling-up was clearly indicated in tablature notation), it is evident that Corkine intended the songs sung with the bass viol alone as simple two-part compositions, without any further harmonic elaboration. In this connexion one may recall that the ayres in Dowland's first book may, according to the title, ' be sung to the Lute, Orpherian, *or* Viol de Gambo'. There can be no doubt that a good deal was left to individual choice and circumstances in this matter of accompaniment. In several of the song-books ayres which are essentially solo songs are described as being ' for two voices ', the bass part, in staff notation, being provided with words, so that it could either be sung or played on the bass viol, or perhaps both sung and played at the same time. In Ford's book there are indications for certain notes to be tied together when played on the viol, though, through syllabic necessity, they would be divided when sung. Corkine's second book, anyway, provides the first English example of songs consisting only of a voice-part and a bass. This later became the universal manner of setting forth songs in print, but, unlike Corkine's, these later songs were designed for harmonic elaboration at the hands of the performer.

Among the instrumental pieces in Corkine's second book is a tune to Marlowe's ' Come live with me and be my love '.

Thomas Ford

Thomas Ford's *Musicke Of Sundrie Kindes* (1607), his only publication, contains ten ayres ' for four voices to the Lute, Orpherian or Bass Viol, with a dialogue for two voices and two Bass Viols in parts, tuned the Lute way '. The second part of the book consists entirely of instrumental music for two bass viols. The songs are similar in character and construction to those of Dowland's first book, and were evidently designed as harmonized tunes which might be sung either by four voices unaccompanied, or by one voice to the lute, with such other voices as might be present ' offering at an inward part '. Two of them, ' Since first I saw your face ' and ' There is a lady sweet and kind ', are so well known as to be almost hackneyed, but they are too often sung from unpleasantly garbled versions. In their original form they have a quiet, simple beauty, though it is difficult to see why they alone should have been singled out for remembrance during the long period when these English ayres were completely neglected, for they are certainly no better than dozens of others of their kind. ' What then is love, sings Corydon ' is a very pretty little song with a marked resemblance to the tune known as ' Barafostus' Dream ', which appears in two settings in the Fitzwilliam Virginal Book.

Ford was in the service of Prince Henry and later of King Charles I. He died in 1648 and was buried at St. Margaret's, Westminster. A set of three manuscript part-books, in a mid-seventeenth-century hand, preserved in the library of Christ Church, Oxford, contains several songs by Ford in what appears to be an arrangement for two tenors and a bass. Amongst them is the only known setting, by any contemporary of Shakespeare, of ' Sigh no more, ladies '.[1] The text as given in the manuscript is not identical with Shakespeare's, but the tune fits Shakespeare's words, and may have been composed for them in a different and more satisfactory form than that in which it appears in the manuscript. This arrangement shows a curious attempt at realism by dividing the first line between two voices thus :

Example 24.

Sigh, sigh,

no more, no more,

---

[1] Published, in solo form, by the Oxford University Press.

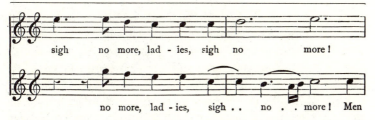

sigh　no　more, lad - ies, sigh　no　　more !

no　more, lad - ies,　sigh . .　no . . more ! Men

But, like other similar realistic touches, it is repeated in the
succeeding verses, where it is entirely inappropriate.

Francis Pilkington

The four-part ayres of Francis Pilkington (1605) are somewhat
akin to those of Ford and of Dowland (in his first book), but they
are considerably less suitable for performance by a solo voice
with the lute. Pilkington was primarily a madrigalist, and many
of his ayres are constructed on solid polyphonic lines. One of
them, ' Down a down, thus Phyllis sung ', seems to have been
intended for a solo voice with three viols, as no words are given
in the three lower voice-parts, except in the refrain, in which
the players may have been expected to join. This procedure is
met with again in Martin Peerson's *Private Musicke* (1620).

Thomas Morley

The only other composer of ayres who also distinguished himself in other fields of vocal composition was Thomas Morley,
whose *First Book of Airs or Little Short Songs to sing and play to
the Lute with the Bass Viol* (1600) is the only book of ayres of
which no copy is now accessible to students. The sole surviving
exemplar, which ought, when it was available, to have been
purchased at any price for the British Museum, passed into the
hands of a rich American, who guards it from all eyes with miser-
like jealousy in a New York cellar, where it has thirty-five copies of
the First Folio edition of Shakespeare and other literary treasures
for its fellow-prisoners. Mr. Robert Steele states in the preface

to his excellent work, *The Earliest English Music Printing* (1903), that his book was held up for a whole year while he vainly attempted to procure photographs of this song-book, and Sir Sidney Lee was refused any information about the Shakespeare Folios when he was conducting his bibliographical researches in connexion with the First Folio Tercentenary in 1923. This book contains the only musical setting of any song from a Shakespeare play that was printed during the poet's lifetime. This is, of course, the setting of ' It was a lover and his lass ', and it is an ironic circumstance that although this is the one song of the period that hundreds of people know who have never heard any other, no correct copy of it, in complete form with its accompaniment, is available in print. A manuscript of 1639, which is preserved in the Advocates' Library in Edinburgh, contains the tune in a version which is substantially the same as that given by Sir Frederick Bridge in his extremely untrustworthy volume of *Shakespeare Songs*. The bass of this published version is said to have been supplied by Professor Wooldridge, who saw the original edition before it left England ; but the rest of the accompaniment has evidently been composed by Sir Frederick Bridge, with his customary lack of taste and complete disregard for the style of the period. But most of the other modern reprints of this song are inaccurate also in respect of the tune, of which they omit the concluding portion with its delightful break of rhythm :

Example 25.

The table of contents of Morley's book is printed in Dr. E. H. Fellowes's *English Madrigal Composers*, from which it is possible, conjecturally at any rate, to identify some of the songs. No. 8 of the twenty-one songs, ' Mistress Mine ', is no doubt the ' Mistress mine, well may you fare ', of which the words, tune, and bass (unfortunately without the lute part) appear in the manuscript known as *Giles Earle's book* ; and Nos. 17 and 18, ' Will ye buy a fine dog ? ' and ' Sleep, slumbering eyes ' may be identical with two anonymous songs beginning with these words which are contained in a manuscript in the library of Christ Church, Oxford. No. 11 alone has been transcribed complete from the original version, and may be found in Arnold Dolmetsch's *Select English Songs and Dialogues of the Seventeenth Century* (though even here one suspects that slight additions to the accompaniment have been made by the editor). No. 7, ' Who is it that this dark night ? ' is no doubt a setting of Sir Philip Sidney's well-known lines, and the texts of Nos. 10 and 12, ' Love winged my hope ' and ' Come sorrow come ', may possibly be the same as those of two songs in Jones's second book.

The loss of this book to English music is nothing short of a calamity, for Morley is one of the most distinguished composers this country has ever produced, and we can see from his ballets and canzonets for unaccompanied voices that his style was admirably adapted for the composition of ayres. Morley arranged the four lower parts of fifteen of his five-part canzonets (published in 1597) for the lute, the tablature appearing, on alternate pages, in the ' Cantus ' part-book of this work. In dedicating the canzonets to Sir George Carey, he says :

' I have also set them tablature-wise to the lute in the Cantus book for one to sing and play alone when your Lordship would retire yourself and be more private : howbeit I wot well your Lordship is never disfurnished of great choice of good voices, such indeed as are able to grace any man's songs.'

But with the exception of ' Said I that Amaryllis ', ' O grief, even on the bud ', and ' Our Bonny-boots could toot it ', it cannot be said that any of the songs are particularly effective in this form, and even these three lose a great deal in the transcription. One or two of the ballets would be much more suitable for singing as accompanied solos, and indeed the tune of ' Now is the month of maying ' does appear with lute accompaniment in Add. MS. 15117 in the British Museum, allied, curiously enough, to Campion's poem, ' The peaceful Western wind '.

A tune which appears (without words) in Morley's *Consort Lessons* under the title ' O Mistress mine ' has been in recent years thought to be a setting of the lyric in *Twelfth Night*, and as such has been reprinted in a very distorted form. There is no authority whatever for associating Shakespeare's poem with this tune ; the words do not even fit the music, which is metrically of a quite different construction.

Example 26.

The tune looks as though it belonged to a five-line stanza with a rhyme-scheme *a-a-b-b-a*, the last three lines being repeated. The words may have been those of a popular song which Shakespeare adapted and made use of as a starting-point for a flight of his own fancy—or, as is far more probable, Shakespeare may have had nothing to do with the matter, and the similarity of title in tune and lyric is mere coincidence. The three words form a natural enough beginning for any number of different songs, and it is by no means unlikely that more than one poet should have made use of them. Morley himself, as we have seen, set to music another poem beginning with the words ' Mistress mine '.

10

Bartlet, Cooper, Maynard, Peerson, Attey, and others

JOHN BARTLET, who describes himself as a ' Gentleman and Practitioner in this art ' (i. e. music), published in 1606 a book of ayres :

' A Booke of Ayres with a Triplicitie of Musicke, Whereof The First Part is for the Lute or Orpharion, and the Viole de Gambo, and 4. Partes to sing, The second part is for 2. Trebles to sing to the Lute and Viole, and third part is for the Lute and one Voyce, and the Viole de Gambo. 1606.'

There is a good deal of very commonplace stuff in this work; but the four-part ' When from my love I look'd for love ' is brisk and crisp when sung with the four voices (though the lute part is shoddy and ill written); the two very indecorous songs, ' A pretty duck there was ' and ' Of all the birds that I do know ' are bright and witty; and the duet for two trebles, 'Whither runneth my sweetheart ? ' is a sheer delight, though it is greatly indebted to Morley's ' It was a lover and his lass '. The book concludes with a long and very dull solo song about birds, with some curious attempts at imitating their calls and cries.

John Cooper

The seventeen published songs of John Cooper (who lived in Italy for a while and changed his name to Coprario) are, with three exceptions, all steeped in heavy gloom. The exceptions are the sprightly ayres in Campion's masque at the marriage of

the Earl of Somerset. His other songs are contained in two
books : *Funeral Tears for the death of the Right Honourable the
Earl of Devonshire,* published in 1606, and *Songs of Mourning :
Bewailing the untimely death of Prince Henry,* printed in 1613.
The songs are for the most part conscientiously well made, with
smooth melodic outlines which sometimes rise to the level of
genuine expressiveness as in ' Oh sweet flower too quickly fading '
from the first book and ' How like a golden dream ' from the
second. But one has only to compare Cooper's ' In darkness
let me dwell ' with the incomparable setting of the same
poem by Dowland, to see how Dowland towered above the
ordinarily good craftsman of his day. A good deal of chamber
music for viols by Cooper is preserved in various manuscript
collections.

The ' Ayres That Were Sung And Played, at Brougham Castle
in Westmerland, in the King's Entertainment ', composed by
George Mason and John Earsden, contain no music of any particular interest except one very robust tune, ' Dido was the
Carthage Queen ', which, however, is less reminiscent of a lutenist's
ayre than anticipatory of some of the popular songs of the mid-
seventeenth century.

The only song-book of the period which is of poor quality
from start to finish, without any redeeming feature except the
amusing words by Sir John Davies which may be found elsewhere, is John Maynard's *The XII Wonders Of The World.*

Robert Dowland

Robert Dowland's
' A Musicall Banquet. Furnished with varietie of delicious
Ayres, Collected out of the best Authors in English, French,
Spanish, and Italian. 1610.'

is a most interesting anthology dedicated to Sir Robert Sidney, who was the compiler's godfather. It contains, in addition to the three songs of John Dowland already mentioned, a very beautiful setting by one Richard Martin of some lines of Robert, Earl of Essex, ' Change thy mind since she doth change ', a charming song by Robert Hales, one of the Grooms of Her Majesty's Privy Chamber, ' O eyes, leave off your weeping ', and songs by Anthony Holborne, Daniell Batchelar, and ' Tesseir ', who is, no doubt, the Charles Tessier whose *Premier livre de chansons et airs de cour* was printed in London by Thomas Este in 1597. Of the foreign songs, by far the most interesting are the two composed by Giulio Romano, better known as Caccini, ' Amarilli, mia bella ' and ' Dove dunque morire '. These had been published by the composer himself in his famous book, *Le nuove musiche*, in 1601, where the vocal line was supported only by a figured bass, to be filled up at the discretion of the performer. In the *Musical Banquet* they are presented, like the English songs, with the harmonic accompaniment fully developed in the lute part, thus providing an admirable example for modern editors who wish to elaborate the figured basses of early seventeenth-century Italian music.

Martin Peerson

Martin Peerson's *Private Musicke, or The First Booke of Ayres and Dialogues* (1620) contains some admirable songs and duets with accompaniment for three viols. In certain numbers the viol parts are provided with the words of refrains to be sung at the end of each verse, as in the ayre of Pilkington referred to above, and in certain songs in Thomas Ravenscroft's *Brief Discourse*. This is the procedure adopted in the lovely lullaby, ' Upon my lap my sovereign sits ', the words of which are by Richard Verstegan, the Roman Catholic priest whom Dowland mentions in his letter to Sir Robert Cecil. There is no part for the lute in this book, but on the title-page Peerson says that the songs ' for want of Viols . . . may be performed to either the virginal or Lute, where the Proficient can play upon the ground, or for a shift to the bass Viol alone '. Thus we see that the practice of playing extempore from a bass alone was already creeping into England. This is the first time that the virginals are mentioned in English music as a suitable instrument for the accompaniment of voices. It has been suggested that, for some reason connected with the tension of the different strings employed, there may have been a difference in pitch between the virginal-tuning and that adopted for the lute and viol in England. In Italy the *gravicembalo* was used for accompanying solos and duets as early as 1571 by Luzzasco Luzzaschi, Maestro de Cappella to the Duke of Ferrara, and in 1600 Luzzaschi published a book of songs for solo voice accompanied by the *gravicembalo*.

John Attey

The last book of airs with lute accompaniment to be published in England was John Attey's

' The First Booke of Ayres of Foure Parts, With Tableture for the Lute : So made, that all the parts, may be plaide together with the Lute, or one voyce with the Lute and Base-Vyoll. 1622.'

In this work the lute part does not double that of the three lower voices so exactly as do the lute parts of Dowland, Jones, and the earlier composers. Attey also provides the only example in the song-books of a purely instrumental prelude to a four-part ayre. Attey, who is described as a ' Gentleman and Practitioner in Music ', tells his patron, the Earl of Bridgwater, that he will consider himself fortunate, ' if I may by this means but vindicate myself from being held a drone in the mellifluous garden of the Muses, and contribute but the smallest drop to the immense ocean of this divine knowledge '.

The book contains some pleasant music with no outstanding qualities save for the last song in the book, ' Sweet was the song the virgin sung ', a flawless work of serene beauty which forms a fitting conclusion to this golden period of English song. Attey achieves many remarkable effects of tone-colour by his careful and original methods of spacing out his chords between the different voices.

For nearly thirty years after the appearance of Attey's book no songs of any importance were published in England (for the so-called *Madrigals and Ayres* which Monteverdi's disciple, Walter Porter, produced in 1632 belonged to a genre quite different from that of the ayres of the lutenists), and by the time Henry Lawes produced his first book of ayres in 1653, the character of English music had undergone a profound change. In these songs we see the great tradition in its decadence and decay. Rhythmic interest has disappeared, the sweeping lines of melody of the older masters have given place to short, halting phrases, and the carefully worked-out accompaniments for lute and viol or for supporting voices are no longer to be found ; the songs are printed with a bass alone.

Some of John Wilson's *Cheerfull Ayres*, published in 1660, date from the early years of the century, but even these have been re-arranged to suit the prevailing taste of the time, and are given in simple three-part harmony without further accompaniment.

II

Ayres in Manuscript Collections

NONE of the original manuscripts of the printed song-books have come down to us ; the only autograph manuscript of a complete book of ayres that has survived is one which, though obviously prepared for the press, was never actually printed. This is the book of *Ayres To be Sunge to the Lute and Base Viole Newly com-*

posed by George Handford, which is preserved in the library of
Trinity College, Cambridge.   It bears a dedication :

' *To the high and mighty Prince, Henry Prince of Wales.*

' Most excellent Prince, give leave to an humble vassal to
prostrate the best of his labours at the foot of your transplendent
greatness.   I bring no wax nor honey to the hive of which the
Almighty hath made your Highness the hopeful stay and comfort.
I only make an unprofitable murmur, living like an idle bee of
others' labours, whilst they laborious are a little refreshed with
the echoes of my harmony and musical endeavours : the best of
which I have selected in humble consecration unto your Highness,
yet fearing my harshness will not arride the ear acquainted with
nothing but super-eminence, on the bowed knee of lowest humility
I crave of your excellence that the submissive devotion of my
uttermost endeavours may not be distasteful.   The Lord Almighty
preserve your Highness' grace to his glory and the eternal good
of the common wealth.

' From Cambridge
' the 17th of December 1609
' Your Highness' most humbly devoted
' George Handford.'

The book contained eighteen songs, of which one is now missing
from the manuscript, and two dialogues.   The music is not
remarkable, and the quality of the poems is noticeably below the
level of that which we are accustomed to find in the song-books
of the lutenists.   The best song in the book is ' Go weep, sad
soul ', in which the composer makes expressive use of augmented
intervals.   It is worth remarking that the book contains no time-
signatures, no examples of triple time, and is barred regularly
throughout, mostly in bars of four minims.

The four finest songs for voice and lute which we have from
manuscript sources are contained in Add. MS. 15117 in the
British Museum.   They are ' Awake, ye woeful wights ', ' O death,
rock me asleep ', ' Willow willow ', and ' Have you seen but a white
lily grow '.   The first three belong to the early years of Elizabeth's

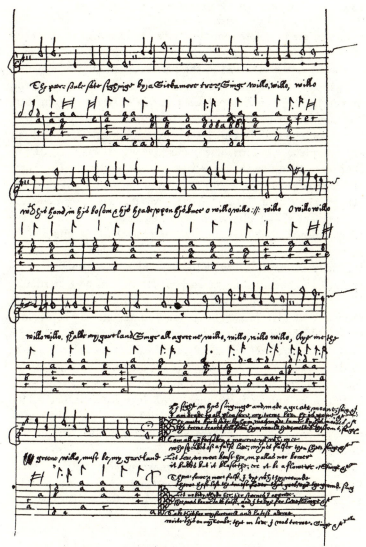

'The Willow Song' from Add. MS. 15117, British Museum.

reign and are therefore some thirty years older than the majority
of the ayres we have been considering. The fourth was evidently
composed at the very end of the period, when Italian influences
were already making themselves felt in English song. The words,
by Ben Jonson, were first published in *The Devil is an Ass* in 1616,
but they may have been written earlier and 'privately imparted'
to the composer. The only lutenist to whose work this song bears
any resemblance is Ferrabosco, and his long association with the
poet lends colour to the conjecture that he wrote it. The words
of ' Awake, ye woeful wights ' are from Richard Edwards's play
Damon and Pithias (1564), and as Edwards was a composer as
well as being a poet, playwright, and Master of the Children of the
Chapel Royal, it is reasonable to suppose that the music is his
also. According to a stage direction in the play, this song was
originally accompanied by the Regal which was a small portable
organ. The poem ' O death, rock me asleep ' has been attributed
both to Anne Boleyn and to her brother Rochford, but it is more
probably, as Mr. Arkwright has suggested, one of the ' death-
songs ' which were a regular feature of the early plays, and which
Shakespeare satirizes in the Pyramus and Thisbe burlesque in
A Midsummer Night's Dream. Two different settings of this
poem have come down to us : one in triple time, constructed on
a kind of ground of three notes, with lute accompaniment, and
the other in common time, for voice and four viols. The text of
the ' Willow Song ' in *Othello* differs but slightly from the text
of this manuscript. Desdemona calls it ' an old thing ', so we may
suppose that it was already well known when the play was produced
in 1604. This song and the lute setting of ' O death, rock me
asleep' might conceivably be the work of Robert Parsons, who
died in 1570.

Other manuscripts of solo songs of considerable importance
are *Giles Earle's book* (Add. MS. 24665, British Museum), and
two manuscripts in the library of Christ Church, Oxford, but

these unfortunately have no tablature for the lute, the only accompaniment indicated being a bass in single notes. Both these books contain copies of songs which are also to be found in the printed song-books, sometimes with interesting textual variations. *Giles Earle's book* contains so many songs of Campion, sometimes with text and music widely different from the version printed by Campion himself, that we may suppose Earle to have been acquainted with a friend of the poet-composer, if not with Campion himself. This book contains Campion's poem, 'What is a day or a month or a year', with its appropriate tune, and two very beautiful lyrics which bear unmistakable signs of being the work of Campion. Each poem is written out under a blank stave of music, as though the copyist had a tune in his head when writing them out, which he meant to transcribe; however, the notes have not been filled in.

The dramatic songs for voice and string-quartet written for the early Elizabethan court plays by Robert Parsons, Richard Farrant, and others hardly come into the category of ayres, for they are constructed on bigger and more definitely polyphonic lines. Of the non-dramatic songs with string-quartet accompaniment the finest is 'When May is in his prime', of which the words, and probably the music, are by Richard Edwards, who died in 1566. From various dates later in the century we have the fresh and delightful cuckoo-songs of Richard Nicholson, organist of Magdalen College, Oxford, and one of the contributors to *The Triumphs of Oriana*; the exquisite lullaby, 'My little sweet darling', by William Byrd; the carol, 'Sweet was the song the virgin sung' (the tune of this song, which bears no resemblance to Attey's setting of the same poem, is also found in William Ballet's lute book, 1594); and some vigorous songs of a humorous nature composed, or perhaps only arranged, by one William Wigthorpe.

I

Some Technical Considerations

THERE is not the slightest evidence to show that Dowland or any of the other song-writers, save Campion, themselves composed the words of the lyrics which they set to music; there is, on the other hand, abundant evidence that they received their verses from others, for many of the poems in the song-books are traceable in the published works of well-known writers of the time, such as Sir Philip Sidney, Ben Jonson, Francis Davison, Anthony Munday, George Peele, Thomas Lodge, and many others.

The song-writers of this period are often praised rather uncritically for their supposedly meticulous regard for the sense and accent of the words they set to music. This attitude is, of course, the result of the reaction against the too strophic methods of the eighteenth and nineteenth centuries. They are sometimes blamed, on the other hand, for doing violence to the verbal accent of the poem, but this, in nine cases out of ten, is due to misunderstanding of the rhythmic principles on which they worked.

The real secret of the Elizabethans' success in welding verbal and musical phrases into a homogeneous whole is to be found in their clear realization of the fact that rhythm and metre are not identical. A metrical stanza may be composed of a number of different rhythmical phrases of varying lengths, but the good speaker of verse will stress the rhythms conditioned by the sense of the words, leaving the metre to the hearer's understanding. Metre is simply a formal framework which when displayed on a printed page makes the construction of the verse immediately clear to the reader. Every English song of the period we are dealing with will be found to be based upon a metrical scheme as precise and regular as that of the poem which prompted it.

By 'regular' I mean that however varied in length and rhythm the phrases composing the metrical stanza may be, the sum total

of beats contained in the stanza will be clearly divisible into regular
sections of three or four beats, according to the time-signature
of the song. These sections are indicated in modern notation by
bar-lines occurring at regular intervals ; but these bar-lines must
not be regarded as having any such accentual significance as the
bar-line acquired at the end of the seventeenth century, and has
retained, to some extent, ever since. The idea of accenting
music by the bar-line was unknown to the Elizabethans, and to
them would have seemed as absurd as the declamation of blank
verse line by line as though it were barred off into so many
feet of long and short syllables, regardless of the sense of the
words and the cadence of phrases.

Madrigals and other unaccompanied vocal music which was
printed in separate part-books were almost invariably unbarred,
and in the lutenist's song-books the barring is usually (though by
no means invariably) irregular and rather haphazard, as though
its only purpose were to keep voice and lute together. In setting
out this music in modern notation for practical use to-day, we
get, paradoxically enough, much nearer to the unbarred freedom
of the original by the insertion of unaccentual bar-lines at regular
intervals, for the sake of clarity and convenience in reading, than
by retaining the conventional association between bar-lines and
strong accents, and barring at irregular intervals determined by
the cadences of separate phrases. No reader of verse would be
in any doubt as to the proper manner of distributing the stresses
and pauses in such a sentence as

> thou shalt not lack
> The flower that 's like thy face, pale primrose, nor
> The azur'd hare-bell, like thy veins, no, nor
> The leaf of eglantine,

and the bar-lines in a passage of this kind are of no more significance to the singer than the division of the verse into lines is to
the actor :

Example 27.

And with blood-y streams of sor-row drowns all our bet - ter deeds.

The arrangement in both cases is designed to appeal to the eye alone, so that the metrical structure of the verse or music may be apparent at every point. Syncopation, as at present understood, is entirely foreign to the music of the madrigalists and lutenists, and such syncopation as appears in modern editions of their work is more apparent than real. Mr. Percival Vivian, in his Introduction to the 'Muses Library' edition of Campion, asserts that Campion's musical setting of 'When thou must home to shades of underground' 'does violence to the verbal accent of the poem in many ways'. But let us take one of the examples he refers to :

Example 28.

To hear the sto - ries of thy fin - ish'd love,

From that . . smooth tongue whose mu - sic Hell can move.

The metre of this passage is quite obviously a regular three beats to a bar ; but if the bar-lines had to indicate the verbal accentuation, the passage would have to be re-arranged thus :

Example 29.

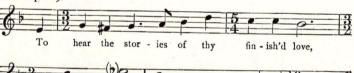

To hear the stor - ies of thy fin - ish'd love,

From that smooth tongue whose mu - sic Hell can move.

How much simpler for the eye is the regular barring (as well as being nearer to Campion's own arrangement), once the principle of accenting by the sense of the words and rhythm of the phrase, and not by the bar-lines, is clearly understood.

Margaret Glyn sums up the matter very clearly in her book, *About Elizabethan Virginal Music,* when she says that ' To get rid of syncopation by changing the length of the bar, and thus altering the accent, is not to give us the Elizabethan effect, which was one of great subtlety. What we need to do is *to get rid of the accent,* not only the actual accent, but the *sense* of accent '— that is, of the sense of quantitative accent. R. O. Morris, in his masterly book on *Contrapuntal Technique in the Sixteenth Century,* pronounces definitely in favour of regular barring in modern editions of Elizabethan music, and his admirable chapter on ' Rhythm ' in this work should be studied by all who wish to arrive at a clear understanding of this somewhat complex question.

The lutenists' ayres were in their day, and still are, music of a simple and popular character ; they should therefore be presented to the modern reader in the clearest and simplest manner that is consistent with absolute accuracy in rendering the notes set down by the composer. They are living music, not resuscitated antiques ; they should therefore be set forth and studied as living music.

There is no advantage in adhering to the obsolete conventions of Elizabethan notation which are likely to confuse the ordinary reader of to-day ; but where notes and text are concerned, nothing should be added to or detracted from what the composer actually wrote. As the Rev. A. Ramsbotham wrote in an excellent article some years ago :

' Every editor of early music should regard himself as a steward of treasure, and is required to be faithful in the way he keeps it or deals it out to others. An editor's first business is to set down the notes he finds written by the composer ; if he does that he is faithful, and very little else will be required of him. . . . In these days of scholarly research the man who proves unfaithful stands condemned. No one would dare to edit Shakespeare or Ben Jonson by replacing the original phrases with modern clichés; he would have the whole world of literary criticism down on him. But something very similar has too often been done to the composers of Elizabethan and Jacobean times, on the plea that " this old stuff won't go down " unless it is dressed and garnished in accordance with modern taste. The truth of the matter is the exact opposite of this. The writers of that day knew their business as well as any modern, and better than most, and they require none of this wrong-headed " editing ".'

That sums up the duties of the modern editor very clearly. The accompaniments originally designed for lute and viol can be transcribed for use on the pianoforte without any alteration of notes whatever. They stand as little in need of alterations or additions as do the accompaniments of the songs of Schubert or Moussorgsky. It has been argued that as these works were conceived long before the tone of the pianoforte was thought of, they should therefore be adapted or modified in some way so as to become suited to ' the idiom of the pianoforte '. But there is no such thing as ' the idiom of the pianoforte '. No musician of good taste would think of ' adapting ' the harpsichord concertos of Mozart in any way before playing them on the pianoforte; indeed, a great deal of their physical charm for modern ears derives from the pellucid clarity of their texture, which is so unlike that of the style of writing that was commonly called ' pianistic ' in the latter half of the nineteenth century. And what common factor is there to the several methods of writing for the piano of such widely different composers as Beethoven, Chopin, Debussy, Bartók, and Sorabji? In any case, an editor's sole business is to produce a clear and accurate *text* of his subject; if the performer wishes to embellish that text, he is at liberty to do so—but such embellishments are rarely successful, save in such exceptional works as Liszt's transcriptions of Schubert's songs and Paganini's Caprices, which we enjoy as one great artist's commentary on the music of another.

If, when we are presented with a plain and accurate text of some old music by an acknowledged master, we find that it offends our ears, we may be very sure that it is our ears that are at fault, and not the old master; to publish the work of an old master with modern additions and 'improvements' is nothing short of an insult to his memory.

There is an admirable poem by Samuel Butler on this subject, and it is pleasant to think of Butler in Elysium, conducting a choir of all the composers of the past whose works have been maltreated by irresponsible editors, in a choral setting of these lines (which were originally prefixed to Butler's cantata 'Narcissus'), slightly adapted to suit the requirements of the particular circumstances:

> May he be damned for evermore
> Who tampers with a printed score;
> May he by poisonous snakes be bitten
> Who writes more parts than what we've written.
> We tried to make our music clear
> For those who sing and those who hear,
> Not lost and muddled up and drowned
> In turgid 'pianistic' sound;
> So kindly leave the work alone
> Or do it as we want it done.

CHRONOLOGICAL TABLE

Showing the principal literary and musical publications from the accession of Queen Elizabeth to the death of John Dowland in their relation to other events. Unless otherwise indicated, the dates given are those of publication, not of performance or composition.

1558 Accession of Queen Elizabeth.

1561 Bacon born.

1562 Norton and Sackville's *Gorboduc* produced. Samuel Danyel born.

1563 John Dowland and Michael Drayton born. The Thirty-nine Articles drawn up.

1564 Shakespeare, Marlowe, and Galileo born. Michael Angelo died.

1565 Tobacco-smoking introduced into England. Pierre Guédron born.

1567 Campion, Monteverdi, and Nashe born. Palestrina's *Missa Papae Marcelli.*

1568 Le Roy and Ballard's *Brief and easy introduction to learn the tableture* published in English.

1571 Whythorne's *Songs of 3. 4. and 5. voices* (containing the first solo song with string-quartet accompaniment published in England).

1572 Massacre of St. Bartholomew in Paris.

1573 Ben Jonson and John Donne born. Christopher Tye died.

1575 Tallis and Byrd granted a twenty-one years' monopoly of music-printing. Tallis and Byrd's joint volume of *Cantiones sacrae.* First public theatre opened in London. Titian died.

1578 Holinshead's *Chronicles*, including Harrison's *Description of England.*

1580 Lyly's *Euphues.*

1583 Orlando Gibbons and Philip Massinger born.

1585 Tallis died.

1586 Sir Philip Sidney died at Zutphen. John Ford (the dramatist) born.

1587 Marlowe's *Tamburlane* produced. Execution of Mary Queen of Scots. Byrd assigns his music-printing monopoly to Thomas Este.

1588 Byrd's *Psalms, Sonnets, and Songs of Sadness and Piety* for five voices. Yonge's *Musica Transalpina* (Book I). Arbeau's *Orchésographie.* Marlowe's *Dr. Faustus.* Defeat of the Spanish Armada.

1589 Byrd's *Songs of Sundry Natures* and *Sacrae Cantiones* (Book I). Henry IV succeeds to the French throne. Kyd's *Spanish Tragedy* produced.

1590 Whythorne's *Duos* for voices or instruments. Watson's *Italian Madrigals Englished* (containing twenty-three madrigals by Marenzio). Sidney's *Arcadia* and Spenser's *Faerie Queene* (Books I–III).

1591 Palestrina's Mass, *Aeterna Christi munera*. Herrick born.

1592 Este's *Whole Book of Psalms*. Monteverdi's *Third Book of Madrigals*. *Arden of Feversham*. Shakespeare's *Henry VI* (*Part I*) produced. Montaigne and Robert Greene died.

1593 Marlowe killed. Shakespeare's *Venus and Adonis* published and *Richard III* produced. George Herbert born.

1594 Morley's *Four-part Madrigals*. Gesualdo's first two books of Madrigals. Palestrina's *Madrigali spirituali*. Mundy's *Songs and Psalms*. Palestrina and Tintoretto died. *Romeo and Juliet* and *The Taming of the Shrew* produced. Nashe's *Unfortunate Traveller*.

1595 Morley's *Ballets* and *Two-part Canzonets*. John Wilson born. Peele's *Old Wives Tale*. *A Midsummer-Night's Dream* produced.

1596 Barley's *New Book of Tablature* (containing the first solo song with lute accompaniment published in England). *The Merchant of Venice* and *Richard II* produced. Henry Lawes born.

1597 Dowland's *First Book of Ayres*. Morley's *Five-part Canzonets* (with alternative versions for voice and lute). Tessier's *Premier livre de chansons et airs de cour*. Morley's *Plain and Easy Introduction to Practical Music*. *Dafne*, an opera by Peri and Caccini, privately performed at Florence. Peele died. *Henry IV* (*Part I*) produced.

1598 Cavendish's *Ayres*. Farnaby's *Canzonets*. Wilbye's *First Set of Madrigals*. Morley obtains a fresh monopoly of music-printing. *Henry IV* (*Part II*) and *Much Ado about Nothing* produced.

1599 Spenser and Marenzio died. John Hilton born. Dekker's *Shoemaker's Holiday*.

1600 Dowland's *Second Book of Ayres*. Jones's *First Book of Ayres*. Morley's *Ayres*. Weelkes's *Five and Six-part Madrigals*. Emilio del Cavaliere's *Rappresentazione di Anima e di Corpo* performed. Artusi's *Delle imperfettioni della moderna musica.* Peri's opera, *Euridice. England's Helicon. As You Like It* and *The Merry Wives of Windsor* produced.

1601 Rosseter's *Ayres.* Jones's *Second Book of Ayres. The Triumphs of Oriana.* Caccini's *Le nuove musiche. Hamlet* and *Twelfth Night* produced. Ben Jonson's *Poetaster.* Nashe died.

1602 Campion's *Observations in the Art of English Poesy* and Samuel Danyel's *Apology for Rime.* Davison's *Poetical Rhapsody.*

1603 Dowland's *Third Book of Ayres.* Gesualdo's *Sacrae Cantiones.* Monteverdi's *Orfeo* produced. Queen Elizabeth and Morley died.

1604 Greaves's *Songs. Othello* and *Measure for Measure* produced. Tessier's *Airs et vilanelles français, italiens, espagnols, suisses et turcqs . . a 3. 4. et 5. parties.*

1605 Hume's *Musical Humours.* Pilkington's *Ayres.* Dowland's *Lachrimae.* Byrd's *Gradualia* (Book I). Heywood's *Rape of Lucrece.* Gunpowder Plot. *King Lear* and *Macbeth* produced.

1606 Danyel's *Songs.* Bartlet's *Ayres.* Cooper's *Funeral Tears. Antony and Cleopatra* produced.

1607 Ford's *Music of Sundry Kinds.* Hume's *Poetical Music.* Campion's *Lord Hayes Masque.* Jones's *Madrigals.* Byrd's *Gradualia* (Book II). Tourneur's *Revenger's Tragedy.*

1608 Jones's *Ultimum Vale.* Monteverdi's *Arianna* performed. Gabriel Bataille's *Airs de differents autheurs* (Book I). Milton born.

1609 Ferrabosco's *Ayres.* Jones's *Musical Dream.* Handford's *Ayres* (MS.). Dowland's *Micrologus.* Wilbye's *Second Set of Madrigals.* Ravenscroft's *Pammelia* and *Deuteromelia.* Shakespeare's *Sonnets. Cymbeline* produced. Dekker's *Gull's Horn-book.*

1610 Robert Dowland's *Musical Banquet.* Corkine's *First Book of Ayres.* Jones's *Muses Garden for Delights. The Winter's Tale* produced.

1611 Maynard's *XII Wonders of the World.* Byrd's *Psalms, Songs, and Sonnets.* Gesualdo's *Fifth and Sixth Books of Madrigals* and *Responsonia. Parthenia,* the first music that ever was printed for the Virginals. Beaumont and Fletcher's *Knight of the Burning Pestle. The Tempest* produced. Ravenscroft's *Melismata.*

1612   Dowland's *Pilgrim's Solace*. Corkine's *Second Book of Ayres*. Orlando
Gibbons's *Madrigals and Motets*. Webster's *White Devil*. Peacham's
Minerva Britannica. *Don Quixote* published in English.

1613   Campion's *First Two Books of Ayres* (?). Cooper's *Songs of Mourning*.
Gesualdo's *Six Books of Madrigals* published in score.

1614   Gesualdo and El Greco died. Ravenscroft's *Brief Discourse* and Leighton's *Tears or Lamentations of a sorrowful soul*. Webster's *Duchess of
Malfi* produced.

1616   Shakespeare and Cervantes died.

1617   Campion's *Third and Fourth Books of Ayres* (?) and *New Way of making
four parts in Counterpoint* (?). Galileo : ' E pur se muove.'

1618   Mason and Earsden's *Ayres*. Execution of Sir Walter Raleigh.

1620   Peerson's *Private Music*. Bacon's *Novum Organum*. Campion died.

1621   Andrew Marvell born.

1622   Attey's *Ayres*. Tomkins's *Songs of 3. 4. 5. and 6. parts*. Peacham's
Compleat Gentleman. Henry Vaughan born.

1623   *First Folio Shakespeare*. Byrd, Rosseter, and Weelkes died.

1625   King James I, Orlando Gibbons, John Fletcher, and Thomas Lodge
died.

1626   Monteverdi's *Combattimento di Tancredi e di Clorinda* produced. Bacon
John Cooper, and John Dowland died.

BIBLIOGRAPHY OF MODERN REPRINTS
OF THE AYRES

J. FREDERICK BRIDGE. *Shakespeare Songs.* (Novello.)

CHARLES VINCENT. *Fifty Shakespeare Songs.* (Winthrop Rogers.)

FREDERICK KEEL. *Elizabethan Love-songs.* Two vols. (Boosey.)

No attempt at fidelity to the original music has been made in these editions. The accompaniments have been entirely re-written in a mid-Victorian style, and even the melodies are not correctly given in many examples.

E. H. FELLOWES. *The English School of Lutenist Song-writers.* (Stainer and Bell.)

This edition 'is planned to produce in complete form the songs of the great Elizabethan and early Jacobean lutenists'. Up to the present (1925), volumes containing songs by Dowland, Rosseter, Campion, Ford, and Pilkington have appeared.

Each song is presented in two forms. First, with the original note-values, time-signatures, and barring, the accompaniment being given both in lute-tableture and in a literal transcription in staff notation (with the addition of phrase-marks which do not appear in the original). The bass-viol part, and, in the case of the four-part ayres, the three lower voice parts, are omitted altogether. (Some of the four-part ayres are, however, published separately, as part-songs.)

In the second version the note-values are generally shortened (minims of the original becoming crotchets, &c.), irregular barring in accordance with the verbal accent, and without any time-signatures, is introduced, and the accompaniments have been entirely re-written, with the addition of preludial bars wherever these do not occur in the original. Expression-marks have been added. In both versions the spelling and punctuation of the poems have been modernized.

PETER WARLOCK and PHILIP WILSON.

    (*a*) *English Ayres* (5 vols.). (Enoch.)

    (*b*) Danyel's *Chromatic Tunes.* (Chester.)

    (*c*) Dowland's *Two songs with violin obbligato from 'A Pilgrim's Solace'.* (Chester.)

    (*d*) *Thirty Ayres suitable for school use in 'The Oxford Choral Songs'.* (Oxford University Press.)

A representative selection of about 150 of the best of the Ayres. While endeavouring to satisfy every reasonable demand of scholarship, the editors have aimed primarily at the production of a popular edition which can be used by any singer without previous knowledge of Elizabethan music or regard for historical considerations. The accompaniments consist of a literal transcription of the lute and bass-viol parts, without any alterations or additions. The note-values have been shortened in many cases, as the minim and semibreve have come to be regarded, in modern times, as long notes associated with slow tempo, whereas to the Elizabethan a minim was, as its name implies, a note of short duration, of approximately the same value as the present-day crotchet. Bar-lines have been inserted at regular points, in accordance with the principles set forth in the last chapter of this book (in which all the musical illustrations are transcribed direct from the original editions). A general indication of pace has been suggested at the beginning of each song, but expression-marks have been left, as the Elizabethans left them, to the taste of the performer. The spelling and punctuation of the poems have been modernized.

PETER WARLOCK.

(*a*) *Four English Songs of the early Seventeenth Century.* (Oxford University Press.)

Four songs from manuscript sources where tune and bass only are given. The accompaniments have been reconstructed as nearly as possible in accordance with the style of the Elizabethan lutenists.

(*b*) *Twenty-two Elizabethan Songs with string quartet accompaniment.* (Oxford University Press.) (3 vols.)

Literally transcribed from manuscript part-books.

(*c*) *Eleven ' Songes of fower and five voyces'* by Thomas Whythorne (1571). (Oxford University Press.)

(*d*) *Forty Elizabethan and Jacobean songs and part-songs* (Curwen).

E. H. FELLOWES's *English Madrigal Verse* (Clarendon Press) is a useful guide to the literary contents of the song-books, but it contains an enormous number of errata.